SITTING in BARS WITH CAKE

AUDREY SHULMAN

SITTING *in* BARS *with* CAKE

**LESSONS AND RECIPES FROM ONE YEAR OF
TRYING TO BAKE MY WAY TO A BOYFRIEND**

ILLUSTRATIONS BY
JENNIFER ORKIN LEWIS

ABRAMS IMAGE, NEW YORK

Editor: Camaren Subhiyah
Designer: Darilyn Lowe Carnes
Production Manager: Anet Sirna-Bruder

Library of Congress Control Number: 2014945996

ISBN: 978-1-4197-1582-2

Text copyright © 2015 by Audrey Shulman
Illustrations copyright © 2015 by Jennifer Orkin Lewis

Printed and bound in the United States
10 9 8 7 6 5 4 3 2 1

Abrams Image books are available at special discounts when purchased in quantity for
premiums and promotions as well as fundraising or educational use. Special editions can also
be created to specification. For details, contact specialsales@abramsbooks.com
or the address below.

THE ART OF BOOKS SINCE 1949

115 West 18th Street
New York, NY 10011
www.abramsbooks.com

DISCLAIMER

The people who appear in this book are based on my sugar-fueled,
alcohol-addled memories of meeting guys in crowded, noisy bars well after my bedtime.
Some recollections may be a little hazier than others, so please excuse any
imprecision and enjoy the show.

For Chrissy and Katy,
who are way better than boyfriends.

CONTENTS

Chapter 4: Fruity

Chapter 5: Savory

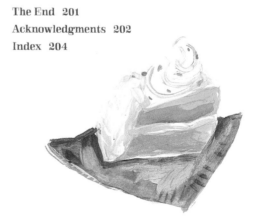

Welcome!

Dear friends,

I'm so delighted you're interested in reading about my year of baking and bar-hopping to bait a boyfriend. Or maybe you're just in the market for new cake ideas. Either way, I hope you'll get a kick out of these retellings and recipes as if you'd been accompanying me on my cake exploits. (I'm sorry we didn't know each other then, or else I would have invited you to join.)

Here are some things you should know:

Before last year, I could probably count the number of beers I'd had on one hand. You'd be more likely to find me making a Jell-O mold than doing Jell-O shots, cohosting murder mystery parties in the comfort zone of my apartment as opposed to driving around Los Angeles at all hours of the night trying to pick up guys in bars. I didn't know how to pick up guys, well, anywhere.

Then one summer, all that changed. My best friend, Chrissy, decided to have her birthday party at a bar, and as the self-appointed baker of our friend group, I brought along a cherry cake I had made from scratch. I was in the middle of cutting and serving pieces for our friends when I looked up to see that all of the guys across the bar were staring at me, and staring at my cake, silently formulating the best way to come over and ask for some. As someone who took prescription medicine for sweaty hands until well after college, this was a rather startling moment of discovery for me.

Holding a cake = guys want to talk to you.

Let me back up just a minute so you can fully grasp the importance of this revelation. I grew up being that girl with bad bangs on the bar mitzvah circuit who no one asked to dance. I never had a straight date to prom and wasted far too many months in college crying over boys who quickly lost interest in me after realizing I was more like a first-grade teacher than a tortured artist with loose morals. I thought maybe my luck would change after graduation, and I'd finally score a boyfriend when I moved to a bigger city and became a more assertive adult. Maybe people would stop giving me grow-a-boyfriend kitsch for Valentine's Day and my aunt would stop sending me dating self-help books. Maybe I would finally connect with the right person and everything would just work out.

So I tried to put myself out there. I went on a flurry of online dates. I let people set me up. I tried dating a friend and even someone from work, but there was never any lasting success. I couldn't tell if I wasn't meeting the right people (maybe) or if something was wrong with me (probably). As much as I didn't want to admit it, there was some ocean-size progress to be made in the getting-comfortable-around-boys department. So that night, as I stood in the bar holding my cake on its flimsy little tray, I had an epiphany.

Homemade cake was the icebreaker of the century.

I could go up to any guy in the bar under the pretense of offering him a slice; it was just like hosting a party at someone else's house. My friends watched as I approached every boy within spitting distance, maintaining previously unimaginable periods of eye contact because now I had a conversation piece, and it didn't really matter if I was blushing because the guys were too busy eating cake to notice.

People go inexplicably insane when offered free dessert.

"You *made* this?!" the boys asked, their mouths full. "Are you an *angel*?!" By the end of that night, I had talked to more guys over cake than I had during the entirety of my undergraduate career. Chrissy joked that all I needed to do to find a boyfriend was bake cakes and go sit in bars. I thought this was hysterical, but not something I could actually go through with. It implied a certain amount of kitchen labor and bravery, not to mention spending more time in the foreign territory of bars.

The rest of the year went by, and I was still single and still tired of it. I really didn't feel like making an online dating profile again and wasn't quite ready to call it quits and throw myself into full-fledged spinsterhood. So in an uncharacteristically brazen disregard for rational action, I decided I would go back to what had worked for me: I would meet guys by taking cakes to bars on a regular and relentless basis. I just wouldn't go to the same bar twice, lest I give up the whole charade.

It sounded like a feasible strategy: bake fifty cakes and take them to fifty bars over the course of a year, offering pieces to potential boyfriends until one surfaced. If I was still single when it was all said and done, at least I would know I had made a pretty valiant effort to not be.

So I did it.

I did it for an entire year, you guys.

I took fifty freaking cakes around town and spent a billion dollars on confectioners' sugar. And now I have eight cavities and a helluva lot of stories to prove it, this book being a collection of my very favorite encounters.

After making it through my dating-permissible years with such a paltry amount of male interaction, here was my marathon of being-with-boys experience. I met dozens of guys in dozens of bars: guys who were sweet, guys who were nuts, guys who asked me to marry them, and guys who were already married to other people. I had set out to find a boyfriend, but I was picking up a whole handbook of information instead—lessons you can only learn at two o'clock in the morning when you're giving out cake for free.

Every single guy I met was teaching me something, whether he wanted any cake or not. For example:

- Male follow-up skills are slower than dial-up.
- Rebounding is for basketball players and Taylor Swift, not you.
- "I'm full" = "I have a girlfriend," because guys are never full.

Sitting in bars with cake meant opening myself up in ways I never had before. (Um, number one being I had to start drinking.) Yes, it was nerve-racking to go up to strangers every single week and offer them cake, and yes, it was embarrassing if they didn't want any or their girlfriends surfaced mid-offer and I had to quietly back away from the table and pretend I was never there. It was disappointing when guys acted interested and I never heard from them again, and even more so when things progressed to dating but still didn't work out. I was also eating millions of calories' worth of cake batter every week and churning out thousands of dirty dishes. But I'd do it all over again. This dating strategy eventually came to feel normal—I even came to love it.

This is my frosting-filled record of the cake-eaters (and a couple non-cake-eaters) I met that year—the guys responsible for the unexpected education that got me to the other side of the being-with-boys department, a new place where I'm happier, savvier, and far more confident. I might even be better at baking.

There are recipes to go along with the stories; I figured you might want to have some cake on hand while you read.

xx
Audrey

Happy reading/
baking/
sugar crashing . . .

GETTING STARTED

Let's get real, people. I'm a home baker. I have zero professional training, which means I'm not above cramming together a crumbly cake in a lasagna pan and covering the evidence with frosting. *I'm pretty sure it will still taste just as good.*

This is great news for you. Even the most inexperienced of bakers should be able to make and enjoy the following recipes without spending their entire weekend (a) hunting for complicated ingredients, (b) slaving over the stove, or (c) popping muscle relaxers.

Here's a supply list to get you started. It covers everything from baking and getting ready to actually serving up cakes in bars, although I would recommend looking through your desired cake's ingredient list before diving in (as some recipes occasionally call for something a little more unusual). Best of luck!

Supplies

unbleached white flour

large eggs

unsalted butter

vanilla extract

granulated sugar

brown sugar

confectioners' sugar

sour cream or Greek yogurt

whole milk (although 2 percent will suffice)

cocoa powder

baby candy bars or cereal for decoration

resilient apron

27 rolls of paper towels

durable sponge

aluminum foil

the Pandora Supremes station

the *Moulin Rouge!* sound track

This American Life podcasts

nail polish (kept a safe distance from the cake)

trail mix/banana chips (for fuel)

ginger ale (for consumption)

plastic forks

paper plates

napkins in a masculine shade (a lot of them)

serving knife

cake carrier

Chapter 1
Sweet

Cakes for Pleasant Surprises, Thoughtful Gestures, and Full-On Victories

Are you in the mood to whip up something sugary and sentimental, even erring on the side of adorable? The following recipes have been baked up to accompany tales of endearing reactions from my male, cake-eating audience. Yep—these are sweet cakes about sweethearts, who (shocker) actually exist on the bar circuit. Hopefully the sugar high will hit right about the time you arrive at a line or two reaffirming that there are, in fact, still scrumptious single boys floating around.

The Guy Who Made Contact with My Mouth

This guy looked kind of like George Stephanopoulos, if George Stephanopoulos was still young and really amazing at Ping-Pong. He'd been playing a rather captivating game of table tennis when I interrupted to see if he'd like my last piece of cake, which he promptly abandoned his opponent to eat.

He turned out to be a nationally ranked athlete from Bulgaria, made especially evident when he threw an arm out to show how much he loved the cake and shot-put my empty cake tray clear across the room. While his opponent stamped his foot waiting for their game to resume, the Bulgarian insisted on feeding me bites of my own cake, taking care to wipe derailed frosting from my mouth. I had just started to get comfortable with the up-close-and-personalness of this gesture when, without any warning, he grabbed my face and kissed me as a thank-you for the unexpected dessert.

There'd always been a certain layer of tentativeness during those rare moments when I'd found myself within feasible make-out distance of any male person's face, so I was grateful to the Bulgarian for finally bursting the personal-space bubble by pulling me in and slobbering on me.

Kissing in bars isn't supposed to look particularly composed.

Sticky Maple Kiss Cake
with Pumpkin Frosting

For athletic foreigners, syrup-loving Vermonters, and boys who work to break long-standing personal-space issues.

For the cake:

1 cup (2 sticks/230 g) unsalted butter, at room temperature
1 cup (220 g) brown sugar
3 large eggs
1 cup (240 ml) maple syrup
½ teaspoon vanilla extract
2½ cups (310 g) all-purpose flour
½ teaspoon salt
2 teaspoons baking powder
½ teaspoon ground ginger
¼ cup (60 ml) milk

For the frosting:

4 ounces (½ block/115 g) cream cheese, at room temperature
3½ cups (350 g) confectioners' sugar, sifted
¼ cup (55 g) pumpkin puree
1 tablespoon maple syrup
Hershey's Kisses, for garnish

To make the cake: Preheat the oven to 375°F (190°C). Butter two 9-inch (23-cm) round cake pans, line the bottoms with rounds of parchment paper, and dust the pans with flour, tapping out the excess.

Beat the butter and brown sugar together until creamy, then add the eggs, one at a time, scraping down the sides of the bowl. Add the syrup and vanilla.

In a separate bowl, combine the flour, salt, baking powder, and ginger.

Working in batches, stir the flour mixture into the butter mixture, alternating with the milk; stir until just combined. Divide the batter between the prepared pans.

Bake for 25 to 30 minutes, or until a toothpick inserted in the center of a cake comes out clean. Let cool for 5 minutes, then loosen the sides with a knife and invert onto wire racks to cool completely. Peel off the parchment and transfer one cake layer to a serving platter.

To make the frosting: Beat the cream cheese with the confectioners' sugar, then add the pumpkin and beat until smooth. Spread some of the frosting over the bottom cake layer, top with the second cake layer, and spread the remaining frosting over the top. Drizzle the syrup over the top and arrange the Kisses around the top border.

The Guy
Who Was
in a Frat

This guy looked fresh out of a fraternity, his spiked hair and bronzy tan betraying a very recent college education's worth of poor decision making. He could have been the national spokesperson for pub crawling, or perhaps an all-inclusive spring break cruise. "You girls are beautiful, but THAT CAKE!" he said, fake falling over. "Nice!!"

As soon as I offered to cut him a piece, Frat Bro's attention quickly turned to my exceptionally pretty best friend. He offered to buy her a drink, but she said no thanks, she didn't drink, and undeterred, he stuck around, eating the cake and asking her a series of questions that revealed a level of perception far exceeding my understanding of frat boy wherewithal. What was the most rewarding part of her job? What did the future of college admissions look like? Did she also research California fault lines?

Thinking it was only right to give him a heads-up, my friend tactfully hinted that she was much older than he was—as in, more than a decade older than he was.

"Well," he said with a shrug, "you're still pretty bangin'," and returned to his table of similarly dressed Malibu Kens. I wondered if I'd been underestimating the capacity for good in all of them.

YOU CAN BOND
WITH FRAT BOYS
OVER MORE THAN
BEER PONG AND
CANCUN.

Sweet Greek Walnut Cake
with Yogurt Frosting

For undergrads, actual Greeks, and those under the impression that they're still entitled to a spring break.

For the cake:

½ cup (1 stick/115 g) unsalted butter, at room temperature
1 cup (220 g) brown sugar
3 large eggs
¾ cup (180 ml) orange juice
1 tablespoon lemon juice
1 tablespoon honey
1 teaspoon vanilla extract
2 cups (250 g) all-purpose flour
1 teaspoon ground cinnamon
2 teaspoons baking powder
½ teaspoon baking soda
½ teaspoon salt
½ cup (120 ml) sour cream
1 cup (125 g) chopped walnuts

For the frosting:

½ cup (1 stick/115 g) unsalted butter, at room temperature
4 cups (400 g) confectioners' sugar, sifted
¼ cup (60 ml) plain Greek yogurt
1 tablespoon orange juice
Chopped walnuts, for garnish

To make the cake: Preheat the oven to 375°F (190°C). Butter two 9-inch (23-cm) round cake pans, line the bottoms with rounds of parchment paper, and dust the pans with flour, tapping out the excess.

Beat the butter and brown sugar together until creamy, then add the eggs, one at a time, scraping down the sides of the bowl. Add the orange juice, lemon juice, honey, and vanilla.

In a separate bowl, combine the flour, cinnamon, baking powder, baking soda, and salt.

Working in batches, stir the flour mixture into the butter mixture, alternating with the sour cream; stir until just combined. Stir in the walnuts. Divide the batter between the prepared pans.

Bake for 25 to 30 minutes, or until a toothpick inserted in the center of a cake comes out clean. Let cool for 5 minutes, then loosen the sides with a knife and invert onto wire racks to cool completely. Peel off the parchment and transfer one cake layer to a serving platter.

To make the frosting: Beat the butter and confectioners' sugar together until smooth, then beat in the yogurt and orange juice. Mix until fluffy and smooth. Spread some of the frosting over the bottom cake layer, top with the second cake layer, and spread the remaining frosting over the top. Garnish with the walnuts around the top border.

The Guy Who Just Got Ditched

This guy wasn't really in the mood for cake. He'd just come from a date that had ended rather abruptly when the girl had a panic attack in the middle of dinner and decided she'd better go home. Catching him in the aftermath was like getting to witness something akin to the beginning of a therapy session, when his boy brain was still processing what had happened and the topic was up for discussion among those of us at the bar.

We tried to talk things out. Was the girl's panic attack real? If it was, was it because she liked him, or was it because she didn't like him? Was she having a bad time and performed her way right out of the restaurant? Maybe she was an aspiring thespian—we would never know.

While he was clearly mystified, this guy was also concerned for the girl, revealing a surprising amount of feeling when he could have just as easily written her off as high maintenance. I told him I hoped he would go out with her again—maybe their second date would be better.

"Yeah, I think maybe I will," he said, and I believed him. Then I tried to peer pressure him into eating some cake, convinced it might actually cheer him up.

Be generous with advice to vulnerable boy strangers.

Chocolate Marshmallow Cake with Southern Comfort Frosting

For those you can force-feed into feeling better.

For the cake:

1 cup (2 sticks/230 g) unsalted butter,
 at room temperature
1½ cups (300 g) sugar
2 large eggs
1 teaspoon vanilla extract
2 cups (250 g) all-purpose flour
½ cup (40 g) unsweetened cocoa
 powder, sifted
¾ teaspoon baking soda
½ teaspoon salt
1 cup (240 ml) milk
2 cups (100 g) mini marshmallows

For the frosting:

½ cup (1 stick/115 g) unsalted butter,
 at room temperature
3 cups (300 g) confectioners' sugar,
 sifted
2 to 3 tablespoons milk
1 to 2 tablespoons Southern Comfort

To make the cake: Preheat the oven to 350°F (175°C). Butter two 9-inch (23-cm) round cake pans, line the bottoms with rounds of parchment paper, and dust the pans with flour, tapping out the excess.

Beat the butter and sugar together until creamy, then add the eggs, one at a time, scraping down the sides of the bowl. Add the vanilla.

In a separate bowl, combine the flour, cocoa powder, baking soda, and salt.

Working in batches, stir the flour mixture into the butter mixture, alternating with the milk; stir until just combined. Stir in the marshmallows. Divide the batter between the prepared pans.

Bake for 25 to 30 minutes, or until a toothpick inserted in the center of a cake comes out clean. Let cool for 5 minutes, then loosen the sides with a knife and invert onto wire racks to cool completely. Peel off the parchment and transfer one cake layer to a serving platter.

To make the frosting: Beat the butter and confectioners' sugar together until smooth, then beat in 2 tablespoons of the milk and 1 tablespoon of the Southern Comfort. Taste and add more Southern Comfort if you'd like, and more milk if the frosting is too thick. Beat until fluffy and smooth. Spread some of the frosting over the bottom cake layer, top with the second cake layer, and spread the remaining frosting over the top.

The Guy
Who Told Me
He'd Send Me
His Recipe

This guy was a real bulldozer of a person, destined for things like heavy lifting and rugby and bodyguarding Britney Spears. When he saw I was carrying a cake into the bar, he pulled out his chair like a real stand-up guy and offered me his table, since there was nowhere else to sit.

We got to talking about cake: what the best kinds were, what kinds I'd baked up recently, and (wait for it) what kinds of cake he liked to make. He worked in construction and, yep, he liked to bake.

"You should make a cheesecake," he said, taking a thoughtful bite from the tiny plastic fork in his enormous hand. "I'll send you my recipe." He started to describe the texture I should be going for—crumbly crust on the bottom, rich filling, maybe some fruit for the very top layer (drool)—but we got separated at some point, and I never did catch him to write it all down.

TOUGH
DUDES
MAY PREFER
BEATING UP
ON BUTTER
AND SUGAR.

White Chocolate Gravel Cheesecake

For gentle giants with excellent manners and anyone harboring slightly to fully realized culinary inclinations.

For the crust:

2 cups (about 22 cookies, 255 g) chocolate sandwich cookies, ground in a food processor, plus 6 more cookies, separated with cream removed, for garnish

¼ cup (55 g) butter, melted

For the filling:

16 ounces (2 blocks/455 g) cream cheese, at room temperature

1 cup (240 ml) sour cream, at room temperature

3 large eggs, at room temperature

½ teaspoon salt

1 cup (6 ounces/170 g) white chocolate chips, melted and kept warm

To make the crust: Combine the cookies and butter in a bowl. Cover and refrigerate for at least 1 hour.

Preheat the oven to 325°F (165°C). Press the cookie mixture into the bottom and up the sides of a 9½-inch (24-cm) pie plate.

To make the filling: Beat the cream cheese, sour cream, eggs, salt, and white chocolate together until the mixture is smooth. Pour into the crust.

Bake for 50 to 60 minutes, until the center is no longer jiggly.

While still warm, place the chocolate cookie wafers around the edge to look like manhole covers. Let cool completely, then refrigerate for at least 2 hours before cutting and serving.

THE ESSENTIAL PLAYLIST

For Baking, Bar-Hopping, and the Subsequent Sugar Coma

(1) "Pumpkin Soup"—Kate Nash (*for the baking part*)

(2) "Country Pie"—Bob Dylan (*for cleaning up while your cake bakes*)

(3) "A Sunday Kind of Love"—Etta James (*for drinking wine while you wait for your cake because it's still not done baking*)

(4) "One Fine Day"—The Chiffons (*for frosting the cake*)

(5) "If You Didn't See Me (Then You Weren't on the Dancefloor)"—Dale Earnhardt Jr. Jr. (*for getting ready*)

(6) "Get Lucky"—Daft Punk (*for driving to the bar*)

(7) "Faded"—soulDecision (*for liquid courage*)

(8) "Single Ladies (Put a Ring on It)"—Beyoncé (*for approaching guys with cake*)

(9) "Don't Leave Me This Way"—Thelma Houston (*for waking yourself up because it's midnight and you're getting tired*)

(10) "Nothing Compares 2 U"—Sinead O'Connor (*for the drive home*)

Bonus Track: "One Less Lonely Girl"—Justin Bieber (*for eating more cake at home before you fall asleep without brushing your teeth or taking out your contacts*)

The Guy Who Proposed

This guy got down on one knee before I really knew what was happening. He had taken one bite of my cake and lowered himself to the floor, proclaiming: "I know we don't know each other very well, but my mom taught me the best way to a man's heart is through his stomach, and, well, this is the best thing I've eaten in two decades."

Considering he was a Christian musician, it must have been too dark in the bar for him to fully register the whole of my eastern European Jewish features.

The photo my friends took at this moment is probably not all that different from one capturing a real proposal. It shows me beaming, blushing, surprised, and my would-be fiancé kneeling, still shoveling in the engagement-worthy cake. Our respective friend groups surround us, huge smiles on their faces, clapping their hands in genuine excitement. While I was fully aware this was all for show, I couldn't help but find the whole display rather enthralling—the declaration of such extreme intentions is really the best compliment you could give to a girl based solely on her baking skills, especially one looking to bait a boyfriend.

You might look just as tasty as the cake you're offering up.

Blushing Berry Cake with Champagne Frosting

For effusive speech-makers at small-scale parties, large-scale celebrations, and major life events.

For the cake:
½ cup (1 stick/115 g) unsalted butter, at room temperature
½ cup (100 g) sugar
3 large eggs
2½ cups (310 g) all-purpose flour
1 (6-ounce/170-g) envelope strawberry Jell-O mix
2 teaspoons baking powder
½ cup (120 ml) milk
1 cup (185 g) diced strawberries and/or whole raspberries

For the frosting:
½ cup (1 stick/115 g) unsalted butter, at room temperature
3 cups (300 g) confectioners' sugar, sifted
3 tablespoons champagne
Sliced strawberries, for garnish

To make the cake: Preheat the oven to 375°F (190°C). Butter two 9-inch (23-cm) round cake pans, line the bottoms with rounds of parchment paper, and dust the pans with flour, tapping out the excess.

Beat the butter and sugar together until creamy, then add the eggs, one at a time, scraping down the sides of the bowl.

In a separate bowl, combine the flour, Jell-O mix, and baking powder.

Working in batches, stir the flour mixture into the butter mixture, alternating with the milk; stir until just combined. Stir in the berries. Divide the batter between the prepared pans.

Bake for 25 to 30 minutes, or until a toothpick inserted in the center of a cake comes out clean. Let cool for 5 minutes, then loosen the sides with a knife and invert onto wire racks to cool completely. Peel off the parchment and transfer one cake layer to a serving platter.

To make the frosting: Beat the butter and confectioners' sugar together, then add the champagne and beat until fluffy and smooth. Spread some of the frosting over the bottom cake layer, top with the second cake layer, and spread the remaining frosting over the top. Garnish with the strawberries on top of the cake.

The Guy
Who Danced
Like No One
Was Watching

These guys were dancing by themselves on an otherwise deserted dance floor—that is to say, they were dancing only and forcefully with each other. The DJ had been playing various hits from the nineties, and these boys were throwing themselves into the music with a resounding level of commitment, a trait fairly hard to come by in would-be boyfriend material.

"Would you guys like some cake?" I yelled over the speakers.

"ABSOLUTELY, WE WOULD LIKE SOME CAKE!" one of them yelled back, and they danced their way over to my picnic table.

To say they were enthusiastic about the cake would be a gross understatement. Their shared adrenaline high from dancing and drinking gave way to loud, impassioned feedback in the form of compliments such as, "This tastes like a gingerbread man crawled into my mouth," and "Jam, cake, frosting—that's my holy trinity."

When I told them I'd made the cake myself, the high-school math teacher of the group got real quiet.

"You don't buy dreams," he told me, shaking his head, "you make them."

I'd be lying if I said I didn't feel compelled to marry him right then and there with Semisonic blasting in the background.

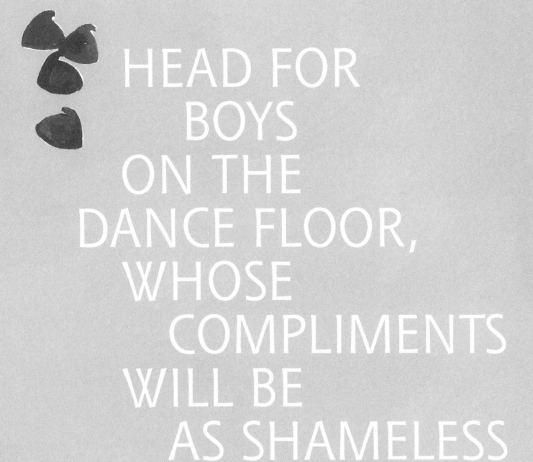

HEAD FOR
BOYS
ON THE
DANCE FLOOR,
WHOSE
COMPLIMENTS
WILL BE
AS SHAMELESS
AS THEIR MOVES.

Dreamsicle Cake with Orange Frosting

For laid-back but confident cake eaters, and guys who wouldn't mind a little Push-Pop stain on their mouths.

For the cake:

½ cup (1 stick/115 g) unsalted butter, at room temperature
1 cup (200 g) sugar
3 large eggs
½ cup (120 ml) coconut oil, melted
½ teaspoon vanilla extract
2½ cups (310 g) all-purpose flour
½ teaspoon salt
½ teaspoon baking powder
½ teaspoon baking soda
1 cup (240 ml) orange juice
1 cup (85 g) sweetened shredded coconut

For the frosting:

½ cup (1 stick/115 g) unsalted butter, at room temperature
4 cups (400 g) confectioners' sugar
2 tablespoons coconut oil, melted
1 teaspoon orange flavoring
1½ tablespoons orange juice
Sweetened shredded coconut, for garnish

To make the cake: Preheat the oven to 375°F (190°C). Butter two 9-inch (23-cm) round cake pans, line the bottoms with rounds of parchment paper, and dust the pans with flour, tapping out the excess.

Beat the butter and sugar together until creamy, then add the eggs, one at a time, scraping down the sides of the bowl. Beat in the oil and vanilla.

In a separate bowl, combine the flour, salt, baking powder, and baking soda.

Working in batches, stir the flour mixture into the butter mixture, alternating with the orange juice; stir until thoroughly combined. Stir in the coconut. Divide the batter between the prepared pans.

Bake for 30 minutes, or until a toothpick inserted in the center of a cake comes out clean. Let cool for 5 minutes, then loosen the sides with a knife and invert onto wire racks to cool completely. Peel off the parchment and transfer one cake layer to a serving platter.

To make the frosting: Beat the butter with the confectioners' sugar, then add the oil, orange flavoring, and orange juice. Beat until fluffy and smooth. Spread some of the frosting over the bottom cake layer, top with the second cake layer, and spread the remaining frosting over the top, and frost the sides. Garnish with the shredded coconut on top of the cake.

The Guy
Who
Didn't Like
Sweets

I met this guy while doling out the worst cake I have ever made. To say it tasted like cough medicine would be more than generous.

We had ended up sitting next to each other at the bar, his friends sharing a table with my friends while everyone drank and ate my terrible cake. I hoped they were all too inebriated to notice it was dry as sand. This guy kept holding his piece of cake without eating any, I assumed because he was enjoying our conversation too much to break away for a fork (and not so much because he sensed the cake was inedible). He seemed so familiar that I worried I had offered him cake before, maybe at another bar, but then attributed this familiarity to our matching levels of questionably extreme friendliness.

I got a message from him a few hours after I left the bar claiming that he was still enjoying my "delicious cake," and another message the next week asking me out for drinks. It was only on the fourth or fifth date that he admitted he wasn't much of a dessert person, and he'd really only taken the cake to talk to me.

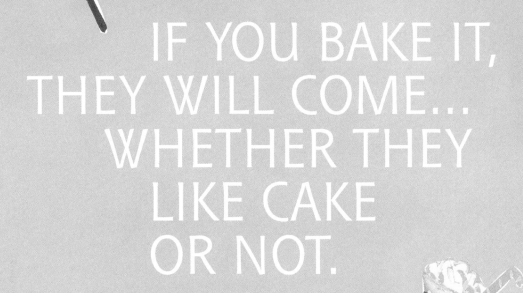

IF YOU BAKE IT,
THEY WILL COME...
WHETHER THEY
LIKE CAKE
OR NOT.

Angel Food Cake with Chocolate-Avocado Frosting

For gentlemen not especially inclined toward dessert, in addition to parties who certainly are.

For the cake:
1 cup (140 g) cake flour, sifted
½ teaspoon salt
1 cup (200 g) sugar
12 large egg whites
1 teaspoon cream of tartar
1 tablespoon honey

For the frosting:
1½ ripe avocados, pureed in a food
   processor
5 tablespoons (25 g) unsweetened
   cocoa powder, sifted
¾ cup (180 ml) honey
1 teaspoon vanilla extract

To make the cake: Preheat the oven to 350°F (175°C).

Combine flour, salt, and ½ cup (100 g) of the sugar and set aside.

In a separate bowl, using an electric mixer with the whisk attachment, whip the egg whites and cream of tartar until foamy. With the mixer running, gradually add the remaining ½ cup (100 g) of sugar, 2 tablespoons at a time, and whip until the whites are glossy, bright white, and hold stiff peaks. Fold in the honey to avoid breaking the peaks.

Remove the bowl from the mixer and use a rubber spatula to gently and quickly fold in the flour mixture. Pour the batter into a tube pan and smooth the top.

Bake for 30 to 35 minutes, or until a toothpick inserted in the center of the cake comes out clean.

Remove from the oven and immediately turn the pan upside-down; if your pan doesn't have feet, try balancing on cans or coffee mugs. An empty wine bottle will also do. Let the cake cool in the pan, upside-down, for at least 2 hours. Remove from the pan and transfer to a serving platter.

To make the frosting: Beat the avocados, cocoa powder, honey, and vanilla together until smooth. Spread over the cooled cake, or serve on the side for dolloping onto slices.

CAN I BUY YOU A DRINK?

Best Booze and Cake Combinations

Chapter 2

Salty

Cakes for Jarring Impressions, Embarrassing Run-Ins, and Conversations with a Kick

For every mortifying moment and misread intention I racked up
during my year of boy baiting, I've created a cake to replicate
that harrowing experience that you can enjoy right here. If you're
looking to serve some dessert with a brackish edge, you can surprise
guests with any of the following recipes that play up the salty and
the sweet. Just comfort yourself with another forkful when you get
to any of the more cringeworthy, pull-the-covers-over-your-head
kind of exchanges I'm forcing you to relive with me.
The dating world can sting, y'all.

The Guy Who Asked If I Was a Grandmother

He and his friends worked on cars for a living, and they were total badasses. They'd come to the bar expressly to drink, not unlike hunters and pirates and men sporting tool belts. This guy had managed to pull off a vest and fedora with his earrings and tattoos, and he wanted to know who exactly had made my cake and why it happened to be in my possession before agreeing to eat any. He insisted I cut him just a tiny piece before he changed his mind and asked for a second, bigger serving.

Soon we were having such a good time together that I let him hold on to my phone while I served more cake, patting myself on the back for infiltrating the cool-kid group by sheer sugary charm. This allowed my new friend ample opportunity to scroll through my current collection of phone photos, which revealed cake picture after cake picture, occasionally interrupted by a guy-eating-cake picture, or a wholesome flower or noteworthy cloud.

"These are all pictures of cake," he said. "Are you a grandmother?"

It only takes one cute guy scrolling through your phone
to totally kill your facade as a cool person.

Peanut Brittle Cake
with Old-fashioned Frosting

For young and old alike, especially young people with old people interests, e.g., puzzles, bridge, and my personal favorite, the domino train game.

For the cake:

1 cup (220 g) brown sugar
¼ cup (60 ml) vegetable oil
4 large eggs
½ cup (120 ml) peanut butter
2 cups (10 ounces/280 g) crushed
    peanut brittle
2½ cups (310 g) all-purpose flour
2 teaspoons baking powder
½ teaspoon salt
½ cup (120 ml) half-and-half

For the frosting:

1⅓ cups (315 ml) heavy whipping
    cream
2 teaspoons brandy
Pinch of salt
Peanuts, for garnish

To make the cake: Preheat the oven to 350°F (175°C). Butter two 9-inch (23-cm) round cake pans, line the bottoms with rounds of parchment paper, and dust the pans with flour, tapping out the excess.

Beat the brown sugar and oil together, then add the eggs, one at a time, scraping down the sides of the bowl. Add the peanut butter and peanut brittle.

In a separate bowl, combine the flour, baking powder, and salt.

Working in batches, stir the flour mixture into the peanut butter mixture, alternating with the half-and-half; stir until just combined. Divide the batter between the prepared pans.

Bake for 35 to 40 minutes, or until a toothpick inserted in the center of a cake comes out clean. Let cool for 5 minutes, then loosen the sides with a knife and invert onto wire racks to cool completely. Peel off the parchment and transfer one cake layer to a serving platter.

To make the frosting: In a chilled bowl, using a chilled whisk or electric mixer with the whisk attachment, whip the cream, brandy, and salt until stiff peaks form. Spread some of the frosting over the bottom cake layer, top with the second cake layer, and spread the remaining frosting over the top. Garnish with peanuts in the center of the cake.

The Guy
Who Liked
to Talk About
Himself

This guy was handsome enough to play Eric in *The Little Mermaid on Ice*. He had just enough remnants of a Southern accent to keep me hanging on every hint of his drawl, and the fact that he wanted a second piece of cake made me want to go home and meet his parents, even if he hadn't bothered to learn my name at any point between our hellos, cake consumption, and closing time.

I kept filling any short silence with another meaningful series of questions about his childhood, his too-recent college experience, and his grand aspirations in the music scene. I let him go on and on about the trials and tribulations of putting together a band. (God, it was so hard to coordinate Skypes with, like, so many people.) He described the album he'd just finished with words like "brutal" and "awesome."

It was only when he started using the word *chick* interchangeably with *girl* that I finally snapped out of it. I'd gotten carried away by his attractive book cover of a face before thinking to open it up and read the first sentence, which upon closer inspection revealed it to be the autobiography of a celebrity mom who overcame adversity by letting herself eat cookies, or something comparably self-focused and of very little interest to me.

Tactfully write off those who missed the boat on social cues.

Bacon Sponge Cake with Potato Chip Frosting

For people who share their own accomplishments without inquiring about any of yours.

For the cake:
10 large eggs
1½ cups (300 g) sugar
3 cups (420 g) cake flour, sifted
½ cup (1 stick/115 g) unsalted butter, softened
1 cup (75 g) crumbled cooked bacon
½ cup (15 g) crumbled potato chips

For the frosting:
2 cups (480 ml) sour cream
½ cup (30 g) finely ground potato chips, plus more for garnish

To make the cake: Preheat the oven to 375°F (190°C). Butter two 9-inch (23-cm) round cake pans, line the bottoms with rounds of parchment paper, and dust the pans with flour, tapping out the excess.

With an electric mixer fitted with the whisk attachment, beat the eggs and sugar together until tripled in volume, about 5 minutes. Gently fold in the flour until just incorporated, then the butter in small increments. Mix in the bacon and potato chips. Divide the batter between the prepared pans.

Bake for 20 to 25 minutes, or until a toothpick inserted in the center of a cake comes out clean. Let cool for 5 minutes, then loosen the sides with a knife and invert onto wire racks to cool completely. Peel off the parchment and transfer one cake layer to a serving platter.

To make the frosting: Whisk the sour cream with the potato chips. Spread some of the frosting over the bottom cake layer, top with the second cake layer, and spread the remaining frosting over the top. Garnish with potato chips on top of the cake.

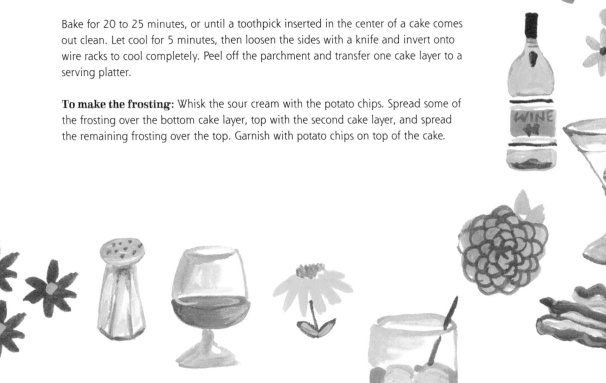

The Guy
Who Claimed
to Be Full

He looked just like the boyfriend I grew up thinking I'd have once I got to high school, thanks to unrealistic expectations built up for me by nineties sitcoms, where everyone seemed to have a handsome, two-dimensional study partner who also asked them to prom. This guy was nothing extraordinary—he just had a nice smile and normal haircut that brought to mind that very fulfilling dating life I'd predicted for my future self as a fifth grader that still had yet to come to fruition.

I walked over and stood next to him at the bar, trying not to look absolutely calculating. I asked what he was ordering before casually segueing into an offer of leftover cake back at my table.

"That's really nice," he said. "But I'm so full. I just came from dinner."

"Are you sure?" I asked. "You could even take some home with you."

"No—thanks, though," he said. "I appreciate it," he added, and turned back to face the bar. I made myself stand still on the off chance he wanted to keep our meaningful conversation going. But after no further acknowledgment on his part, I retreated to my table, feeling slighted and ten years old again.

"He's not really full," my friend said when I relayed what had happened. "He must have a girlfriend."

We realized that guys could eat cake even if they'd just polished off an entire bar mitzvah buffet; they powered through fullness. Turning down cake under the pretense of being too stuffed was really the nicest way possible of saying "closed for business."

"I'M FULL" =
"I HAVE A
GIRLFRIEND,"
BECAUSE GUYS
ARE NEVER FULL.

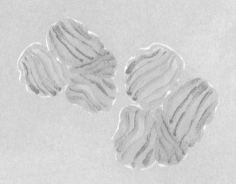

Chocolate Prune Cake
with Salty Frosting

For guys you have no intention of dating and guys who have no intention of dating you.

For the cake:

1 cup (2 sticks/230 g) unsalted butter,
  at room temperature
1 cup (220 g) brown sugar
3 large eggs
1 cup (240 ml) prune baby food (about
  five 2½-ounce/71-g containers)
2½ cups (310 g) all-purpose flour
¾ cup (60 g) unsweetened cocoa
  powder, sifted
2 teaspoons baking powder
½ teaspoon baking soda
½ teaspoon salt
1 cup (240 ml) sour cream

For the frosting:

1½ cups (360 ml) heavy whipping
  cream
¼ teaspoon sea salt

To make the cake: Preheat the oven to 375°F (190°C). Butter two 9-inch (23-cm) round cake pans, line the bottoms with rounds of parchment paper, and dust the pans with flour, tapping out the excess.

Beat the butter and brown sugar together until creamy, then add the eggs, one at a time, scraping down the sides of the bowl. Add the prune baby food.

In a separate bowl, combine the flour, cocoa powder, baking powder, baking soda, and salt.

Working in batches, stir the flour mixture into the butter mixture, alternating with the sour cream; stir until just combined. Divide the batter between the prepared pans.

Bake for 30 to 35 minutes, or until a toothpick inserted in the center of a cake comes out clean. Let cool for 5 minutes, then loosen the sides with a knife and invert onto wire racks to cool completely. Peel off the parchment and transfer one cake layer to a serving platter.

To make the frosting: In a chilled bowl, using a chilled whisk or electric mixer with the whisk attachment, whip the cream and salt until stiff peaks form. Spread some of the frosting over the bottom cake layer, top with the second cake layer, and spread the remaining frosting over the top.

The Guy Who Got Handsy

Full disclaimer: This was my first and only time peddling cake at a wedding, as I'd actually been asked to bring a dessert.

This guy was part of the wedding party, which made him seem deceptively adorable. We'd been seated near each other at dinner and reconnected in the dessert line several hours later, what must have been several drinks later for him. I offered to cut him a piece of my cake, not registering the extent of his drunkenness until he started to cram frosting into his mouth with the hand-eye coordination of a high chair–constricted infant. I watched him, fascinated, this odd combination of sloppiness and formal wear as he sucked down a few more messy bites. He reached for me, and the beginnings of a hug turned into some serious inappropriateness as he announced, "It's just salt in the salt shaker."

"What does that even mean?" I asked, and extricated myself to seek out other, more-composed cake eaters. This guy proceeded to get so drunk that he passed out on the couch outside the banquet hall, where wedding guests stopped to pose for pictures with him on their way out the door. We were all left guessing what exactly he'd meant by his enigmatic salt shaker comment on our drive back home. Was I the salt? Was he the salt?

No, we decided. He was just abominably trashed.

Don't trust the groomsman; he's out to do
every bad thing the groom just signed away.

Bear Claw Cake with Drippy Caramel Frosting

For clumsy dinner guests who you know will have too much to drink.

For the cake:
1 cup (2 sticks/230 g) unsalted butter,
   at room temperature
1 cup (200 g) sugar
3 large eggs
2 cups (250 g) all-purpose flour
½ cup (170 g) almond meal
   or pulverized almonds
2 teaspoons baking powder
½ teaspoon salt
½ cup (120 ml) sour cream
1½ cups (135 g) sliced almonds

For the frosting:
½ cup (1 stick/115 g) unsalted butter,
   at room temperature
1 cup (220 g) brown sugar
¼ cup (60 ml) milk, plus more if
   needed
2 cups (200 g) confectioners' sugar,
   sifted

To make the cake: Preheat the oven to 375°F (190°C). Butter and flour a 12-cup (2.8-L) Bundt pan, tapping out the excess.

Beat the butter and sugar together until creamy, then add the eggs one at a time, scraping down the sides of the bowl.

In a separate bowl, combine the flour, almond meal or almonds, baking powder, and salt.

Working in batches, stir the flour mixture into the butter mixture, alternating with the sour cream; add the sliced almonds and stir until just combined. Pour the batter into the prepared pan and smooth the top.

Bake for 45 minutes, or until a toothpick inserted in the center of the cake comes out clean. Let cool for 5 minutes, then loosen the sides with a knife and invert onto a wire rack to cool completely. Transfer to a serving platter.

To make the frosting: Melt the butter and brown sugar in a medium saucepan over low heat, stirring to combine. Add the milk. Increase the heat to medium and bring to a boil; boil for 1 minute, then remove from the heat and add the confectioners' sugar. You may need to add 1 to 2 tablespoons more milk to make the frosting extra smooth. Immediately pour the hot frosting over the cooled cake.

LURING BOYS WITH SUGAR

The ~~Do's and~~ Don'ts of Sitting in Bars with Cake

(1) Don't bake cakes with polarizing ingredients.

(2) Don't wear dry-clean only.

(3) Don't bring along friends with alcohol problems.

(4) Don't sit with your back to the door.

(5) Don't leave the cake covered up.

(6) Don't assume the bar just happens to have a cake knife.

(7) Don't cut your pieces too small (or too big!).

(8) Don't leave without enjoying a piece yourself.

(9) Don't forget to give the bouncer a piece on your way out.

(10) Don't go to the same bar twice, lest you give up the whole charade!

The Guy
Who Inhaled
The Cake

This guy's right arm was in a sling. He'd been sitting alone watching the football game on TV before he slid over to join me and my friend.

"I only end up here if my night's gone really horribly wrong," he said.

"What happened?" we asked.

He wouldn't say. He was too busy eyeing our cake.

I asked if he wanted a piece, and he gladly took some, wielding the fork in his opposite, unhindered hand. He had nearly finished scarfing down the entire slice before he stopped to ask me what kind of cake it was that he was eating.

It was now clear that putting a great deal of thought into the cake presentation had been unnecessary; the flavors, the decorations, and any ingredients to give the cake a more alluring kind of appeal had gone partially if not completely unnoticed by male cake-eaters. They just heard "cake," and they were in.

DON'T
WASTE TIME
MAKING FOOTBALLS
OUT OF FONDANT
BECAUSE
GUYS WILL EAT
WHATEVER IS
IN FRONT
OF THEM.

Sloppy Joe Cake with Cracker Jack Frosting

For guys who would probably fail to notice if your cake was uncooked, overcooked, or actually a pie in disguise.

For the cake:

½ cup (1 stick/115 g) unsalted butter, at room temperature
1 cup (220 g) brown sugar
3 large eggs
2 cups (250 g) all-purpose flour
½ cup (50 g) finely ground pretzels
2 teaspoons baking powder
1 cup (240 ml) beer
2 cups (80 g) cocoa cereal
½ cup (120 ml) peanut butter

For the frosting:

1½ cups (360 ml) heavy whipping cream
3 cups (200 g) pulverized Cracker Jacks or salted caramel popcorn

To make the cake: Preheat the oven to 375°F (190°C). Butter and flour a 12-cup (2.8-L) Bundt pan, tapping out the excess.

Beat the butter and brown sugar together until creamy, then add the eggs, one at a time, scraping down the sides of the bowl.

In a separate bowl, combine the flour, pretzels, and baking powder.

Working in batches, stir the flour mixture into the butter mixture, alternating with the beer; stir until just combined.

In a separate bowl, mix the cereal and peanut butter together until the cereal is uniformly coated. Spread half of the cake batter in the prepared pan, then spread the cereal and peanut butter mixture over the top. Spread the remaining cake batter over the filling, smoothing the top.

Bake for 35 to 40 minutes, or until a toothpick inserted in the center of the cake comes out clean. Let cool for 5 minutes, then loosen the sides with a knife and invert onto a wire rack to cool completely. Transfer to a serving platter.

To make the frosting: In a chilled bowl, using a chilled whisk or electric mixer with the whisk attachment, whip the cream and Cracker Jacks until stiff peaks form. Spread over the cooled cake, or serve on the side for dolloping onto slices.

The Guy
Who Was
Married

This guy was sitting with a big group of friends, telling a story in a Sean Connery accent. It took me a whole round of cake distribution to realize he was legitimately Scottish, and his table was full of expats.

Maybe it's because Europeans have a more significant pub culture than we do, or maybe it's just because they're better at socialized drinking, but I was very quickly welcomed into their merry clan. The Scotsman exuded the same level of warmth and inclusion as a Tennessee church picnic, and I thought maybe I could fit right in. Maybe his people could become my people. Maybe I could work my way to dual citizenship, even if he was starting to go gray.

The Scotsman declared my baking was so good that he would leave his wife and son for me, who I then found out not only existed but were drinking within earshot—to my great surprise, a son old enough to be a viable dating candidate for me.

While I'd approached these endeavors with an attitude of all-inclusiveness, I hadn't exactly intended to attract married men with adult sons. No harm had been done, of course, just some cultural discussions over cake consumption, but it was a valuable warning for the future.

*Don't get carried away by dreams of dual citizenship
until you know the guy is looking for a mutual return.*

Great Scot Skirlie Cake
with Toffee Frosting

For tea parties, European tourists, and married company partial to oats.

For the cake:
½ cup (40 g) rolled oats
½ cup (1 stick/115 g) unsalted butter,
    at room temperature
1½ cups (330 g) brown sugar
4 ounces (½ block/115 g) cream
    cheese, at room temperature
3 large eggs

2 cups (250 g) all-purpose flour
2 teaspoons baking powder
½ teaspoon salt

For the frosting:
1 cup (240 ml) heavy cream
½ cup (15 g) pulverized toffee bars

To make the cake: In a small saucepan, combine the oats and 1 cup (240 ml) of water and cook over medium heat until the oats are soft and thickened, 7 to 10 minutes. Set aside to cool completely.

Preheat the oven to 375°F (190°C). Butter and flour a 12-cup (2.8-L) Bundt pan, tapping out the excess.

Beat the butter and brown sugar together until creamy. Beat in the cream cheese, then add the eggs, one at a time, scraping down the sides of the bowl.

In a separate bowl, combine the flour, baking powder, and salt.

Working in batches, stir the flour mixture into the butter mixture, alternating with the cooled oatmeal; stir until just combined. Pour the batter into the prepared pan and smooth the top.

Bake for 35 to 40 minutes, or until a toothpick inserted in the center of the cake comes out clean. Let cool for 5 minutes, then loosen the sides with a knife and invert onto a wire rack to cool completely. Transfer to a serving platter.

To make the frosting: In a chilled bowl, using a chilled whisk or electric mixer with the whisk attachment, whip the cream and toffee bars until stiff peaks form. Spread over the cooled cake, or serve on the side for dolloping onto slices.

The Guy
Who Acted
Interested

He was by far the most thrilled person I had ever offered cake to. "This is the nicest thing anyone's ever done for me," he gushed. (That is, my offering him a piece of cake in a bar for free.)

He was so charismatic, I thought maybe I should start bringing him along on future cake outings for morale; with his energy and little-boy face, he seemed more like a cheerful sidekick than a romantic prospect. I was just about to run this idea by him when he looked me in the face and said, "I'm really interested in dating you."

"Oh," I said, taken aback, wondering how this could possibly be the case, not remembering this was the goal of the entire project.

"Are you not available?" he asked.

"No, yes, I'm available," I said, and gave him my number, supremely flustered.

I talked myself into believing I could handle someone this spry, who was clearly several years younger than I was and not completely jaded by the privileged troubles of living in L.A. yet. After worrying that our mutual cheerfulness would turn dark and competitive, I decided that I should still go out with him. No one ever came right out and announced they were interested in dating you, and that directness was worth a lot.

I never heard from him again.

MALE
FOLLOW-UP SKILLS
ARE SLOWER
THAN
DIAL-UP.

Pretzel Roulette Cake
with Pistachio Filling

For bouncy company and young adults prone to rash declarations and changing their minds.

For the cake:
½ cup (100 g) sugar
3 large eggs
1 cup (125 g) all-purpose flour
½ cup (50 g) finely ground pretzels
1 teaspoon baking powder
¼ cup (60 ml) plain yogurt
1 tablespoon finely ground pistachios

For the filling:
¾ cup (180 ml) heavy whipping cream
3 tablespoons finely ground pistachios
⅛ teaspoon salt
1 tablespoon confectioners' sugar

To make the cake: Preheat the oven to 375°F (190°C). Line a 9-by-12-inch (23-by-30-cm) baking sheet with waxed paper or parchment paper.

Beat the sugar and eggs together until foamy.

In a separate bowl, combine the flour, pretzels, and baking powder.

Add the flour mixture to the sugar mixture, then add the yogurt, then the pistachios. Spread the batter into the prepared sheet.

Bake for about 10 minutes, or until the consistency is firm and cakelike.

Have a clean, damp kitchen towel ready for when you take the cake out of the oven. Slide the cake, still on the paper, onto the towel. Starting from a short side, roll the cake up, still on the paper, and wrap it in the towel, forming a roll. Let cool for 30 minutes.

To make the filling: In a chilled bowl, using a chilled whisk or electric mixer with the whisk attachment, whip the cream, pistachios, and salt until stiff peaks form. Unroll and unwrap the cake, being careful not to tear it. Spread the filling over the flattened cake, then roll it back up and transfer to a serving platter, seam-side down. Dust with the confectioners' sugar.

HAVEN'T WE MET?

Commonly Encountered Boy Personalities

(1) The Artist Wearing an Old Man Sweater

(2) The Guy Trying to Pull Off a Shark-tooth Necklace

(3) The Proselytizing Nonprofit Worker

(4) The Affable Musician Who Works Part-time at Starbucks

(5) The Guy Who Invests in Business Models You Don't Understand

(6) The Guy Who Just Wants to Go Home

(7) The Skeptical Skinny Freelancer

(8) The Eccentric Guy Who Works at the Farmers' Market

(9) The Guy Who Dives Right in to Sober Karaoke

(10) The Schmoozy Hollywood Guy with Veneers

Chapter 3

Bitter

Cakes for Crushing Losses, Sour Realizations, and Frustrated Efforts

There's no other way to say it: these are cakes for eating your feelings. They've been paired with my accounts of promising interactions gone wildly astray. This is your go-to chapter for moping, mourning, and commiserating with cake during times of disillusionment, but you're going to have to rejoin society once the tartness wears off. Sometimes you just have to get back in the kitchen and crank out another cake to take to a bar.

The Guy Who Said You'll Never Meet Anyone in This Town

This gentleman was English, which made him seem especially authoritative when he started dispensing unprompted dating advice over cake.

"Los Angeles is a terrible place to meet people," he said.

"Why do you say that?" I asked.

"Because the number one emotion in this town is desperation," he said. "Look around."

We took in the crowd: lots of hot people hoping to get noticed by other hot people who could maybe get them a better job. I had managed to forget that this was the same population that made up my dating pool, and remembering this was not only troubling, but I, too, now seemed just as desperate as these schmoozers in my so-called desperation to bait a boyfriend. My very cake reeked of despondency.

It was only later when comfort-eating cake in the laptop glow of Netflix that I considered I could still meet someone normal. Young people who flocked to big cities had great ambitions and some notion of a work ethic, and I probably wanted to date someone who had plans for their life past living in their parents' basement. I wasn't desperate to find a boyfriend—I was just being proactive about it.

THE DATING
SCENE IN L.A.
IS A SPECIAL
KIND OF
HUNGER GAMES.

Skinny Espresso Cake, No Whip

For actors and model friends who can smell a piece and feel almost as if they ate some.

For the cake:
¾ cup (1½ sticks/170 g) unsalted
    butter, at room temperature
1 cup (200 g) sugar
4 large eggs
2 cups (250 g) all-purpose flour
2 tablespoons instant espresso powder
1 teaspoon baking powder

½ teaspoon baking soda
½ teaspoon salt
1 cup (240 ml) sour cream
¾ cup (125 g) bittersweet chocolate
    chips

To make the cake: Preheat the oven to 375°F (190°C). Butter and flour a 12-cup (2.8-L) Bundt pan, tapping out the excess.

Beat the butter and sugar together until creamy, then add the eggs, one at a time, scraping down the sides of the bowl.

In a separate bowl, combine the flour, espresso powder, baking powder, baking soda, and salt.

Working in batches, stir the flour mixture into the butter mixture, alternating with the sour cream; stir until just combined. Stir in the chocolate chips, then pour into the prepared pan and smooth the top.

Bake for 40 to 45 minutes, or until a toothpick inserted in the center of the cake comes out clean. Let cool for 5 minutes, then loosen the sides with a knife and invert onto a wire rack to cool completely. Transfer to a serving platter.

The Guy
Who Came
with a
Party Bus

This guy was the ringleader of his group, or at least its most sober representative. He had led an entire party bus full of guys wearing ugly Christmas sweaters into the bar, who now swarmed the karaoke machine and were revving up to perform. "I apologize in advance for us," he said. "Please let me know if we get too loud."

I couldn't believe my luck—someone conscientious and down for dressing up. I asked if he wanted a piece of cake.

"You're so nice to ask," he said. "But I'm going to get a drink. We're only at our first stop of the night." He gestured toward the rest of his party bus mates, already in the throes of *NSYNC.

"Are you sure you wouldn't like a small piece? Maybe one for later?" I asked.

"No, thank you," he said, not unkindly. "Thank you so much for asking anyway."

This genuinely polite dismissal set the tone for the rest of the night; not one of these guys in Santa sweaters wanted any cake, and they were all so flipping nice about it. I rotated around the bar to a chorus of well-meaning *no-thank-you*s and *I-really-appreciate-it*s. Who were these gracious boys, and why weren't they hungry? I thought surely their zeal for karaoke would die down and they'd find their way over to our table. They'd grow to want cake. They'd want to talk to us. The strategy would work.

It didn't. They were still singing "Bye Bye Bye" when we left the bar.

The bonds of brotherhood can prevail over even the
most worthwhile of distractions, i.e., cute girls and cake.

Gin and Tonic Cake with Lime Zest Frosting

For those inclined to drink or eat away their sorrows.

For the cake:

½ cup (1 stick/115 g) unsalted butter, at room temperature
1 cup (200 g) sugar
2 large eggs, separated
Grated zest of 1 lemon
Grated zest of 1 lime
¼ teaspoon cream of tartar
2 cups (250 g) all-purpose flour
½ teaspoon baking soda
½ teaspoon salt
½ cup (120 ml) gin
½ cup (120 ml) 7UP

For the frosting:

1½ cups (360 ml) heavy whipping cream
2 tablespoons gin
1 teaspoon tonic
1 tablespoon lime juice
1 teaspoon vanilla extract

To make the cake: Preheat the oven to 375°F (190°C). Butter two 9-inch (23-cm) round cake pans, line the bottoms with rounds of parchment paper, and dust the pans with flour, tapping out the excess.

Beat the butter and sugar together until creamy, then add the egg yolks, one at a time, scraping down the sides of the bowl. Add the lemon and lime zests.

In a separate bowl, using an electric mixer fitted with the whisk attachment, whip the egg whites and cream of tartar together until soft peaks form; set aside.

In another bowl, combine the flour, baking soda, and salt.

Working in batches, stir the flour mixture into the butter mixture, alternating with the gin and 7UP; stir until just combined, then gently fold in the whites until all the ingredients are thoroughly incorporated. Divide the batter between the prepared pans.

Bake for 25 to 30 minutes, or until a toothpick inserted in the center of a cake comes out clean. Let cool for 5 minutes, then loosen the sides with a knife and invert onto wire racks to cool completely. Peel off the parchment and transfer one cake layer to a serving platter.

To make the frosting: In a chilled bowl, using a chilled whisk or electric mixer with the whisk attachment, whip the cream, gin, tonic, lime juice, and vanilla until stiff peaks form. Spread some of the frosting over the bottom cake layer, top with the second cake layer, and spread the remaining frosting over the top and sides.

The Guy
Who Criticized
the Cake

It's only about once a year that I become deeply, unreasonably enraged. My blood gets hot, my thought process turns hazy, and I feel like taking a baseball bat to something and destroying all the goodwill I've built up during two decades of otherwise benevolent behavior.

This was a really close call.

The guy seemed nice enough in the beginning; he'd even offered to buy me a drink. He had just started eating the cake when I did something odd, which was ask him how it was. I never did this. Usually, people knew to say something positive about the cake almost immediately after accepting it; it was the unspoken understanding that came along with eating homemade dessert in front of the person who had slaved over it.

"The frosting is good," he said. "But the cake is a little dry."

I thought maybe I should set down my cake knife and walk away. I thought maybe I should dump a glass of ice water on my head to prevent an outburst. Perhaps it was my duty to pull this guy outside and gently break it to him that this was the absolute worst thing you could tell a baker, that he and his friends should probably leave now before things got ugly. But I didn't say anything.

I managed to change the subject and keep myself from breathing fire, although anything else we talked about that night has been completely forgotten in the aftermath of that dry cake comment, a real culinary affront after all the hours it took to bake the cake, frost it, and strategize the serving of it to people like him.

People who say your cake is dry are dead to you.

Olive Oil Cake with Sesame Seed Frosting

For people who don't appreciate your job performance, housekeeping, or toils in the kitchen. On second thought, don't offer them cake at all.

For the cake:
1 cup (200 g) sugar
3 large eggs
¾ cup (180 ml) olive oil
⅓ cup (75 ml) lemon juice
2 cups (255 g) all-purpose flour
2 teaspoons baking powder
¼ teaspoon baking soda
½ teaspoon salt

For the frosting:
1½ cups (360 ml) sour cream
2 tablespoons tahini
Pinch of salt
2 teaspoons honey (optional)
¼ cup (35 g) sesame seeds, toasted
  and cooled

To make the cake: Preheat the oven to 350°F (175°C). Butter and flour a 12-cup (2.8-L) Bundt pan, tapping out the excess.

Beat the sugar and eggs together until foamy. Beat in the oil and lemon juice.

In a separate bowl, combine the flour, baking powder, baking soda, and salt.

Working in batches, stir the flour mixture into the sugar mixture and stir until well-combined, then pour into the prepared pan and smooth the top.

Bake for 40 to 45 minutes, or until a toothpick inserted in the center of the cake comes out clean. Let cool for 5 minutes, then loosen the sides with a knife and invert onto a wire rack to cool completely. Transfer to a serving platter.

To make the frosting: Whisk together the sour cream, tahini, salt, and honey, if using, then stir in the sesame seeds. Spread over the cooled cake, or serve on the side for dolloping onto slices.

CAKE FAILS AND FIXES

From One Scattered Baker to Another

(1) Crumbly cake?

Transfer cake to a lasagna dish, patting down evenly, and spread frosting over the top when cooled. Pretend this was your intention all along.

(2) Frosting melting off your (still piping hot) cake?

Throw cake in the freezer until chilled (not frozen), and apply a second layer of frosting before you leave the house.

(3) No egg beater to whip cream?

Bring whipping cream, bowl, and whisk to bar, and ask a guy you like to help out by taking a turn beating the cream. (Make sure you wrap the whipping cream in several plastic bags en route to the bar, or you could have a catastrophe.)

(4) Sink hole in the middle?

Cover up holes and uneven spots with frosting whenever possible—even if it means buying (forgive me) canned frosting to keep up appearances.

(5) Ran out of time to bake?

Make frosting and apply to store-bought cake. NO ONE HAS TO KNOW.

(6) Ice cream cake melting everywhere?

Serve cake in tiny cups with spoons. Ask bartender for extra napkins, because you will most definitely run out.

(7) Almost out of cake but a whole truckload of cute guys just walked in?

Cut the pieces smaller and serve on napkins, without forks—if people are eating with their hands, they won't notice the difference in size.

(8) No ingredients for frosting?

Use jam or yogurt in between the layers.

(9) No decorative props or frosting to write with?

Place a single berry on top, or line the border with nuts or cereal.

(10) Cake too dry?

Spread a thin layer of peanut butter or Nutella on each piece.

The Guy Who Was Recently Dumped

It took us a minute to recognize each other. I'd only known him as the boyfriend of an old acquaintance, occasionally exchanging quick how-are-yous when I first moved to L.A. Now here he was with a bunch of single guys, a category I assumed he had fallen into, as his girlfriend was nowhere to be found and he looked stoned out of his mind.

"Sure, I'll have some cake," he said blurrily. He wasted no time telling me that the girlfriend had very recently broken things off. "I'm just torn up about it," he said, taking a big bite, trying to keep it together. The buddies who'd brought him to the party stood nearby listening, on guard to prevent a total meltdown. I worried they'd been through this many times.

I expressed how sorry I was that things hadn't worked out and tried to change the subject. "How's your job going? Are you still working for the soil company?"

"There was never a soil company," he said. "I just made that up. I was growing pot."

"Oh," I said.

"I always thought you were cute," he admitted, pointing his fork in my direction. "Hey, you should give me your info. We should hang out sometime," he decided, his bloodshot eyes perking up.

As sweet as he was, as bad as I felt for him, and as flexible as I'd become in my post-college adulthood to maybe accept pot growing as a current career choice, I knew better than to express interest in someone who was clearly still reeling from a difficult breakup. I asked for his number instead, but haven't gotten around to calling.

REBOUNDING IS FOR BASKETBALL PLAYERS AND TAYLOR SWIFT—NOT YOU.

Bitter Chocolate Dumped Cake with Cheap-Wine Frosting

For post-breakup consumption, catered to your tastes and your tastes alone—you deserve whatever you want.

For the cake:

1 (15.25-ounce/432-g) package
  chocolate cake mix**
3 large eggs
½ cup (120 ml) sour cream
8 ounces (225 g) bittersweet chocolate,
  melted
¼ teaspoon salt
¾ cup (180 ml) wine or alcohol of
  your choice
1 cup (40 g) of your favorite sugary
  cereal, just for kicks

For the frosting:

½ cup (1 stick/115 g) unsalted butter,
  at room temperature
3½ cups (350 g) confectioners' sugar,
  sifted
⅓ cup (30 g) unsweetened cocoa
  powder, sifted
⅓ cup (75 ml) wine

To make the cake: Preheat the oven to 375°F (190°C). Butter and flour a 12-cup (2.8-L) Bundt pan, tapping out the excess.

Dump all the ingredients except the cereal into a bowl and beat together until smooth. Stir in the cereal. Pour into the prepared pan and smooth the top. (Or I mean, you could just eat the batter raw if it will make you feel better. In which case, leave out the eggs.)

Bake for 35 to 40 minutes, or until a toothpick inserted in the center of the cake comes out clean. Let cool for 5 minutes, then loosen the sides with a knife and invert onto a wire rack to cool completely. Transfer to a serving platter.

To make the frosting: Beat the butter and confectioners' sugar together until smooth, then beat in the cocoa powder and wine until fluffy and smooth. Spread over the cooled cake.

**Not a choice; cake mix required. You have to go the easiest route here. You're making this in a Bundt pan expressly because you're too depressed getting over your breakup to have to wash an additional cake pan.

The Guy Who Used My Nose as a Pickup Line

We'd already given this guy a piece of cake earlier in the night, but he'd reappeared, this time with an intentional coat of frosting on his nose.

"Are you Jewish?" he asked me.

"No," I said, confused. "Well, technically, no. Why?"

"I just couldn't help but notice your nose," he said.

Just to give you a nice visual here, my nose is unmistakably prominent, slightly crooked, and alarming when photographed from the side.

"Are you a plastic surgeon?" I asked.

"No, I'm a single Jewish man," he said, and plopped down next to me.

All this time I had thought pickup lines were supposed to give you some kind of confidence boost, or at least opt you in to some hormonally charged banter that resulted in a handful of lusty dates. The fact that this guy had sought me out with some kind of strategy involving frosting on his face was vaguely flattering, but I was fairly relieved to discover pickup lines were nothing to write home about.

Pickup lines should be relegated to the online purgatory of OkCupid.

Chocolate Poppy Seed Cake with Chocolate Frosting

For guys who are unskilled at telling jokes, reading the room, or psyched about Jewish baking.

For the cake:

1 cup (2 sticks/230 g) unsalted butter,
    at room temperature
1 cup (200 g) sugar
8 ounces (1 block/225 g) cream cheese,
    at room temperature
3 large eggs
4 ounces (115 g) bittersweet chocolate,
    melted
2 cups (255 g) all-purpose flour
½ cup (70 g) poppy seeds (not in syrup)
2 teaspoons baking powder
½ teaspoon salt
½ cup (120 ml) milk

For the frosting:

½ cup (1 stick/115 g) unsalted butter,
    at room temperature
3½ cups (350 g) confectioners' sugar,
    sifted
Pinch of salt
½ cup (40 g) unsweetened cocoa
    powder, sifted
½ cup (120 ml) milk

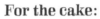

To make the cake: Preheat the oven to 375°F (190°C). Butter two 9-inch (23-cm) round cake pans, line the bottoms with rounds of parchment paper, and dust the pans with flour, tapping out the excess.

Beat the butter and sugar together until creamy, then beat in the cream cheese. Add the eggs, one at a time, scraping down the sides of the bowl. Stir in the chocolate. In a separate bowl, combine the flour, poppy seeds, baking powder, and salt.

Working in batches, stir the flour mixture into the butter mixture, alternating with the milk; stir until just combined. Divide the batter between the prepared pans.

Bake for 25 to 30 minutes, or until a toothpick inserted in the center of a cake comes out clean. Let cool for 5 minutes, then loosen the sides with a knife and invert onto wire racks to cool completely. Peel off the parchment and transfer one cake layer to a serving platter.

To make the frosting: Beat the butter, confectioners' sugar, and salt together until smooth, then beat in the cocoa powder and milk until fluffy and smooth. Spread some of the frosting over the bottom cake layer, top with the second cake layer, and spread the remaining frosting over the top and sides.

The Guy
Who Was
Engaged

Being nice to a girl in a bar when you're engaged isn't necessarily wrong, even if you go so far as to eat a piece of her cake and tell her how much you like it. But maybe when you actually write down your phone number for her after she asks for it under the guise of going to one of your stand-up shows, that's when things get dicey. I mean, should guys start wearing engagement rings? Watches? Baseball caps reading I'VE PROPOSED TO SOMEONE ELSE?

The thing is, I didn't know this guy was engaged. There I was, having a big time chatting with him over cake, privately registering that he fell into both of my ideal personality types (friendly, and friendly with glasses). I laughed when he mentioned doing stand-up about girls taking cakes to bars.

"Why don't you give me your number?" I asked. "I'll go watch you perform sometime." He wrote his number down for me on a valet ticket and left with his buddies, waving good-bye.

My friend allowed me to bask in the glow of my small victory for a moment before gently bursting my bubble. "He told me he thought you were really cute," she said. "He said if he wasn't marrying someone else, he'd be interested in dating you."

"So this means the only number I've gotten tonight belongs to someone who's engaged to another person and unavailable. Yes?"

"Yes, that would be correct."

I guess he was just a guy who thought I genuinely wanted to go hear him do stand-up sometime and contribute to his acting career, which was not exactly the case.

NETWORKING TRUMPS NUPTIALS.

Hidden Layer Chocolate-Raspberry Torte

For people who may neglect to mention important attachments and obligations, e.g., marriage plans, children, or an upcoming incarceration.

For the cake:

8 ounces (225 g) bittersweet chocolate, chopped
½ cup (1 stick/115 g) unsalted butter, at room temperature
½ cup (100 g) sugar
4 large eggs
½ teaspoon salt
1 cup (165 g) raspberries
4 ounces (½ block/115 g) cream cheese, at room temperature
1 tablespoon confectioners' sugar
Raspberries, for garnish

To make the cake: Preheat the oven to 350°F (175°C). Line the bottom of a 9-inch (23-cm) springform pan with a round of parchment paper.

Put the chocolate in a heatproof bowl and set it over a saucepan of simmering water; stir until the chocolate is almost melted, then remove the bowl from the saucepan and stir until smooth. Let cool to lukewarm.

Beat the butter and sugar together until creamy, then add the eggs, one at a time, scraping down the sides of the bowl. Add the salt and cooled chocolate.

In a food processor, puree the raspberries and cream cheese together until smooth.

Spread half of the batter in the bottom of the prepared pan, then spread the cream cheese mixture over the batter as evenly as possible. Gently spread the remaining batter on top.

Bake for about 50 minutes, or until the center is firm and a toothpick inserted in the center of the cake comes out with a few damp crumbs clinging to it. Let cool for 5 minutes, then loosen the sides with a knife and remove the side of the springform pan. Let cool completely. Keeping the pan bottom on for stability, transfer to a serving platter. Sift the confectioners' sugar over the cooled torte and garnish with raspberries.

The Guy Who Knew Too Much

I have a dangerously heightened and healthy sense of modesty when it comes to interpreting male interest, but I'm pretty sure this guy and I were trying to pick each other up.

He was holding a beer in each hand, in town from San Francisco for a ball game with some friends. I thought he was precious, albeit a little drunk for a Thursday night, but whatever he lacked in sobriety he made up for in charm—he was, after all, in sales. We chatted and ate cake while I polished off a Moscow Mule, loosening up enough to casually mention my real reason for inviting him back to the table—a big reveal I hoped he would find rather winning since we were already getting along so well. I knew immediately that this had been a mistake, recognizing flickers of confusion and displeasure registering through his beer haze.

"You could have just come talked to me without cake," he slurred. "I'm ma-a-ad."

I tried to throw together something about the importance of having an icebreaker, that this wasn't a trick, that I genuinely thought he was great, but it was no use. I had blown my chance for not only the beginnings of an impractical long-distance relationship, but continuing our good rapport for the remainder of the evening. I don't think he was actually angry; I think he just felt used.

DON'T SHARE
YOUR DATING
STRATEGY
WITH SOMEONE
YOU WANT
TO DATE.

Orange-You-Glad-We-Met Marmalade Cake with Marmalade Glaze

For friends, frenemies, or romantic prospects who might need an apology.

For the cake:

½ cup (1 stick/115 g) unsalted butter
1 cup (200 g) sugar
3 large eggs
¾ cup (180 ml) marmalade
2½ cups (310 g) all-purpose flour
1 teaspoon baking powder
½ teaspoon baking soda
½ teaspoon salt
½ cup (120 ml) orange juice

For the glaze:

½ cup (120 ml) marmalade
2 tablespoons vodka

To make the cake: Preheat the oven to 375°F (190°C). Butter and flour a 12-cup (2.8-L) Bundt pan, tapping out the excess.

Beat the butter and sugar together until creamy, then add the eggs, one at a time, scraping down the sides of the bowl. Add the marmalade.

In a separate bowl, combine the flour, baking powder, baking soda, and salt.

Working in batches, stir the flour mixture into the butter mixture, alternating with the orange juice; stir until just combined. Pour the batter into the prepared pan and smooth the top.

Bake for 35 to 40 minutes, or until a toothpick inserted in the center of the cake comes out clean. Let cool for 5 minutes, then loosen the sides with a knife and invert onto a wire rack to cool completely. Transfer to a serving platter.

To make the glaze: In a small saucepan, combine the marmalade and vodka and cook over low heat until the marmalade has melted. Pour over the cooled cake and let the glaze set.

PICKUP LINES I WISH
NEVER HAPPENED

(1) "This place has got a really good nonfiction section."

(2) "I saw your posture and something told me I just had to talk to you."

(3) "You're as fine as [expletive]."

(4) "You do know what that Rihanna song is about, right?"

(5) "I steal people's information for a living. But, like, not in an illegal way."

(6) "I'm really interested in dating you."

(7) "I just couldn't help but notice your nose."

(8) "Do you and your friends want to come back to my place? [seeing I was frightened] I mean, my backyard?"

(9) "I'm here to solve the mystery of how you and I are going to go on a date together."

(10) "It's a good thing we aren't married, because you'd never see me."

Chapter 4

Fruity

Cakes for Inappropriate Times, Unlikely Scenarios, and Ridiculous Company

This next batch of cakes highlight the more erratic dealings of my late-night bar excursions with boys—they're the kinds of recipes you should fix up when you're wondering what just happened, and why do things like this keep happening to me? I've made them to commemorate the eccentrics, cake-eaters who surfaced at odd times and in even odder circumstances. They're whimsical desserts for whimsical company, an unpredictable spin on after-dinner fare.

The Guy
Who Had
Mermaid Hair

We weren't sure where exactly he'd come from; he looked like he was about fifteen years old and shouldn't have been allowed in the bar. I'd never seen a guy with hair quite like this, the kind of wavy blond Barbie frizz that I grew up wanting, and still kind of want. It was as though Sean Penn's *Fast Times* character and Daryl Hannah from *Splash* had had a baby right around Y2K and now here he was at our table, quietly eating a piece of cake with a skateboard in his lap.

I tried to ask questions without sounding like a babysitter. Where was he from? What were his interests? Where were his parents, and were they aware he smelled like pot?

"I haven't gotten sick in seven years," he suddenly volunteered.

"What?" we asked.

"I got bitten by a brown recluse three times yesterday, and I was fine."

"But how do you know that?" we asked.

"I just did," he said.

Our attempts at further conversation fell flat, which I chalked up to teenage shortcomings in social situations that don't pertain to selfies or smartphones or being mad about something. He left without saying good-bye, I suppose to go home and avoid his math homework or make electronic music—whatever it is the frustrated millennials do these days.

Be aware: your cake will attract misfit toys.

(Let's Get) Baked Apple Granola Cake with Honey Frosting

For underage hippies and skateboard punks on the go.

For the cake:

3 large apples, peeled, cored, and
  cut into small cubes
1 cup (220 g) brown sugar
1 teaspoon ground cinnamon
¼ teaspoon freshly grated nutmeg
1 cup (2 sticks/230 g) unsalted
  butter, at room temperature
3 large eggs
⅓ cup (75 ml) honey
2 cups (250 g) granola
2½ cups (310 g) all-purpose flour
2½ teaspoons baking powder
½ teaspoon baking soda
½ teaspoon salt
½ cup (120 ml) sour cream

For the frosting:

½ cup (1 stick/115 g) unsalted
  butter, at room temperature
4 cups (400 g) confectioners' sugar,
  sifted
3 tablespoons milk
3 tablespoons honey
1 teaspoon ground cinnamon
Sliced apples, for garnish

To make the cake: Preheat the oven to 375°F (190°C).
Butter two 9-inch (23-cm) round cake pans, line the bottoms
with rounds of parchment paper, and dust the pans with flour,
tapping out the excess.

Toss apples with ½ cup (110 g) of the brown sugar, the
cinnamon, and the nutmeg and set aside.

Beat butter and remaining ½ cup (110 g) of the brown sugar
together until creamy, then add the eggs, one at a time,
scraping down the sides of the bowl. Add honey, then granola.

In a separate bowl, combine the flour, baking powder, baking
soda, and salt.

Working in batches, stir the flour mixture into the butter
mixture, alternating with the sour cream; stir until just
combined. Stir in apple mixture. Divide batter between the
prepared pans.

Bake for 30 to 35 minutes, or until a toothpick inserted in the
center of a cake comes out clean. Let cool for 5 minutes, then
loosen the sides with a knife and invert onto wire racks to cool
completely. Peel off the parchment and transfer one cake layer
to a serving platter.

To make the frosting: Beat the butter and confectioners'
sugar together until smooth, then beat in the milk, honey,
and cinnamon until fluffy and smooth. Spread some of the
frosting over the bottom cake layer, top with the second cake
layer, and spread the remaining frosting over the top. Garnish
with sliced apples.

The Guy
Who Invited
Me Back
to His Place

This guy was from that recently formed tribe of eccentric IT geniuses with heightened mannerisms. He'd pressed both of his hands into my face upon finishing his first piece of cake and exclaimed, "You have such deep dimples!" He wasn't even drunk; he was just completely, certifiably bonkers.

He was eager to show me pictures of his seven hundred nieces and nephews on his iPhone before moving on to a series of a horse and donkey he'd just seen in the desert. "See? They're friends!" he said, pointing to his cracked screen.

"Is it ironic that you're an IT guy and your phone is cracked?" I asked.

"No." He shook his head. "I prefer things that are broken."

He shared some of his other philosophies with me, which involved a focus on being creative in temporary moments and not believing in the necessity of best friends. He even invited me back to his place—er, the backyard of his place—the first and only time this ever happened, which I for safety reasons declined.

ONLY GO HOME
WITH PEOPLE
YOU'VE
GOOGLE-
CONFIRMED
AREN'T SERIAL
KILLERS.

Chocolate-Bananas Cake with Chocolate-Coconut Frosting

For the brilliantly insane or insanely brilliant, e.g., IT whizzes with contradictory belief systems.

For the cake:
½ cup (1 stick/115 g) unsalted butter,
    at room temperature
1 cup (200 g) sugar
2 large eggs
2 (½ cup, 130 g) ripe bananas, mashed
1 teaspoon vanilla extract
2½ cups (310 g) all-purpose flour
¾ cup (60 g) unsweetened cocoa
    powder, sifted
2 teaspoons baking powder
½ teaspoon baking soda
½ teaspoon salt
1 cup (240 ml) sour cream
1 cup (85 g) sweetened shredded coconut

For the frosting:
½ cup (1 stick/115 g) unsalted butter,
    at room temperature
1 tablespoon coconut oil
2 (½ cup,130 g) ripe bananas, mashed
3 cups (300 g) confectioners' sugar, sifted
½ cup (40 g) unsweetened cocoa
    powder, sifted
1 cup (85 g) sweetened shredded
    coconut, plus more for garnish
Sliced banana, for garnish

To make the cake: Preheat the oven to 375°F (190°C). Butter two 9-inch (23-cm) round cake pans, line the bottoms with rounds of parchment paper, and dust the pans with flour, tapping out the excess.

Beat the butter and sugar together until creamy, then add the eggs, one at a time, scraping down the sides of the bowl. Add the bananas and vanilla.

In a separate bowl, combine the flour, cocoa powder, baking powder, baking soda, and salt.

Working in batches, stir the flour mixture into the butter mixture, alternating with the sour cream; stir until just combined. Stir in the coconut. Divide the batter between the prepared pans.

Bake for 25 to 30 minutes, or until a toothpick inserted in the center of a cake comes out clean. Let cool for 5 minutes, then loosen the sides with a knife and invert onto wire racks to cool completely. Peel off the parchment and transfer one cake layer to a serving platter.

To make the frosting: Beat the butter, oil, bananas, and confectioners' sugar together until smooth, then beat in the cocoa powder and coconut until fluffy. Spread some of the frosting over the bottom cake layer, top with the second cake layer, and spread the remaining frosting over the top and sides. Garnish top of the cake with sliced banana and sprinkle shredded coconut around the bottom of the cake.

The Guy
Who Licked
Elizabeth's Leg

This guy kept asking my friend Elizabeth to dance, and she kept politely declining. Not only was he not really her type (as in tall, dark, and passably normal), but also there was no music to dance to. He was the drunkest person we'd ever encountered at a bar. He might also have been the oldest.

We gave him a piece of cake to pacify him, which he ate at the end of our tiny table, swaying to an imaginary beat. He stopped suddenly to bend down, what we both assumed was a motion to pick up cake crumbs from the floor, but Elizabeth's appalled face suggested he'd had other intentions for ducking under the table.

I nearly fell out of my chair shooing him away, pushing him back in the direction of the pool tables. "Thanks for coming by! Enjoy the cake!" I said, waving, as we watched him stumble toward the door.

"That dude just licked my ankle," Elizabeth groaned. "A well-adjusted person would have screamed. I guess I'm just not a well-adjusted person."

While she wins some award for enduring the grossest act committed by a cake-eater, we both learned not to give drunk middle-aged people we felt sorry for cake as a goodwill gesture.

There are limits to hospitality with strangers.

Puckering Lime Cake with Sour Frosting

For sour candy fans or people who have just suffered through a rather sour experience.

For the cake:
½ cup (1 stick/115 g) unsalted butter,
   at room temperature
1 cup (200 g) sugar
1 cup (240 ml) frozen limeade
   concentrate, thawed
2 large egg whites
¼ teaspoon cream of tartar
2½ cups (310 g) all-purpose flour
2 teaspoons baking powder

½ teaspoon baking soda
½ teaspoon salt
½ cup (120 ml) plain yogurt

For the frosting:
1 cup (240 ml) heavy whipping cream
1 tablespoon lime juice
Strips of lime, for garnish

To make the cake: Preheat the oven to 375°F (190°C). Butter two 9-inch (23-cm) round cake pans, line the bottoms with rounds of parchment paper, and dust the pans with flour, tapping out the excess.

Beat the butter and sugar together until creamy, then add the limeade.

Using an electric mixer with the whisk attachment, whip the egg whites and cream of tartar until soft peaks form and set aside.

In another bowl, combine the flour, baking powder, baking soda, and salt.

Working in batches, stir the flour mixture into the butter mixture, alternating with the yogurt; stir until just combined. With a rubber spatula, gently fold in the egg whites until thoroughly incorporated. Divide the batter between the prepared pans.

Bake for 30 to 35 minutes, or until a toothpick inserted in the center of a cake comes out clean. Let cool for 5 minutes, then loosen the sides with a knife and invert onto wire racks to cool completely. Peel off the parchment and transfer one cake layer to a serving platter.

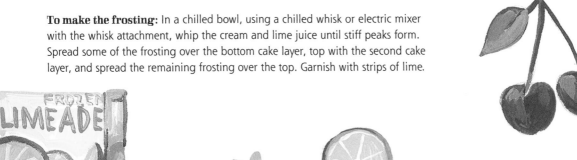

To make the frosting: In a chilled bowl, using a chilled whisk or electric mixer with the whisk attachment, whip the cream and lime juice until stiff peaks form. Spread some of the frosting over the bottom cake layer, top with the second cake layer, and spread the remaining frosting over the top. Garnish with strips of lime.

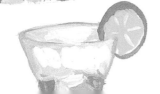

MEMORABLE CAKE REJECTIONS

(1) "I just opened my beer."

(2) "We just spent three hours at Souplantation."

(3) "I'm more of a pie person."

(4) "Can you get that off of our table?"

(5) "I'm allergic to pumpkin."

(6) "I just came from a party with cake."

(7) "It's gym day."

(8) "I'm an alcoholic."

(9) "I'm not exactly a chocolate guy."

(10) [Too intoxicated to formulate answer.]

The Guy Who Thought This Was an Art Project

He'd noticed me rotating around the bar for the past hour or so, doling out cake to strangers before making my way to his table. "I love you and what you're about," he said, gesturing toward me and my handful of plastic forks. It was the equivalent of a sophisticated high-five from one aesthete to another.

It took me a moment to realize that he was under the impression that my cake-related actions were solely in the name of art.

We were in the type of place where it wouldn't have been unreasonable for a girl to be offering cake as a creative endeavor; most of the other patrons were ethereal hipsters in overalls or couples in head-to-toe vintage discussing the current crisis in Syria. Ke$ha had just walked out of a corner room.

Perhaps this guy imagined I would return home and put together a found object installation based on my experiences that night, or make a three-dimensional pie chart out of discarded food and videotape myself eating it the next day for breakfast. He wasn't seeing this for the endgame that it was, which, while imaginative, was really just about finding someone to make out with on a regular basis.

The assumption was flattering; not only did I seem wildly creative, but also maybe I wasn't looking as suspicious as I thought.

You may find yourself in an unintentional performance piece.

Sangria Party Cake
with Triple Sec Frosting

For sculptors, dancers, interdisciplinary artists, or anyone who looks like they belong in a Free People catalog.

For the cake:
½ cup (1 stick/115 g) unsalted butter,
   at room temperature
1 cup (200 g) sugar
3 large eggs
2 tablespoons lime juice
½ teaspoon orange flavoring
2½ cups (310 g) all-purpose flour
2 teaspoons baking powder
½ teaspoon baking soda
½ teaspoon salt
½ cup (120 ml) red wine

For the frosting:
½ cup (1 stick/115 g) unsalted butter,
   at room temperature
3 cups (300 g) confectioners' sugar,
   sifted
3 tablespoons triple sec

To make the cake: Preheat the oven to 375°F (190°C). Butter two 9-inch (23-cm) round cake pans, line the bottoms with rounds of parchment paper, and dust the pans with flour, tapping out the excess.

Beat the butter and sugar together until creamy, then add the eggs, one at a time, scraping down the sides of the bowl. Add the lime juice and orange flavoring.

In a separate bowl, combine the flour, baking powder, baking soda, and salt.

Working in batches, stir the flour mixture into the butter mixture, alternating with the wine; stir until just combined. Divide the batter between the prepared pans.

Bake for 20 to 25 minutes, or until a toothpick inserted in the center of a cake comes out clean. Let cool for 5 minutes, then loosen the sides with a knife and invert onto wire racks to cool completely. Peel off the parchment and transfer one cake layer to a serving platter.

To make the frosting: Beat the butter and confectioners' sugar together until smooth, then beat in the triple sec until fluffy and smooth. Spread some of the frosting over the bottom cake layer, top with the second cake layer, and spread the remaining frosting over the top.

The Guy
Who Directed
Adult Films

We should have known something was off by the mustache, but then again, most guys are currently sporting this same sign of bad judgment if they've recently purchased a bike or want in on the L.A. improv scene.

The guy in question seemed normal enough by cake-eater standards, gaining some credibility upon mentioning he went to an East Coast school and asking a couple of courteous questions; he even had some nice things to say about the cake. I was just starting to warm up to his bad 'stache and girl jeans when what he did for a living came up.

"I'm an adult film director," he said, nodding, and took another bite of cake. It was as though he had just told us he was a speech therapist or an accountant, or ran the pretzel kiosk at the mall, as though this particular line of work was so in keeping with contemporary societal norms that it required no further explanation or disclaimer.

"Do you enjoy your work?" one of my friends asked politely, not missing a beat.

I'm not sure how fulfilling this guy found his current career path to be, as I managed to black out during his answer and came to while ordering a virgin mojito.

YOU CAN ALWAYS LEAVE THE CAKE BEHIND.

Seedy Cherry Cocktail Cake with Brandy Frosting

For guys inclined toward mixed drinks or those whose work you find to be generally squalid.

For the cake:

½ cup (1 stick/115 g) unsalted butter,
    at room temperature
1½ cups (300 g) sugar
3 large eggs
½ teaspoon vanilla extract
2 cups (300 g) cherries, halved and
    pitted
2½ cups (310 g) all-purpose flour
2 teaspoons baking powder
½ teaspoon salt
6 tablespoons (90 ml) brandy
¼ cup (60 ml) milk

For the frosting:

½ cup (1 stick/115 g) unsalted butter,
    at room temperature
4 cups (400 g) confectioners' sugar,
    sifted
2 to 3 tablespoons brandy
2 to 3 tablespoons milk

To make the cake: Preheat the oven to 375°F (190°C). Butter two 9-inch (23-cm) round cake pans, line the bottoms with rounds of parchment paper, and dust the pans with flour, tapping out the excess.

Beat the butter and sugar together until creamy, then add the eggs, one at a time, scraping down the sides of the bowl. Add the vanilla, then the cherries.

In a separate bowl, combine the flour, baking powder, and salt.

Working in batches, stir the flour mixture into the butter mixture, alternating with the brandy and milk; stir until just combined. Divide the batter between the prepared pans.

Bake for 25 to 30 minutes, or until a toothpick inserted in the center of a cake comes out clean. Let cool for 5 minutes, then loosen the sides with a knife and invert onto wire racks to cool completely. Peel off the parchment and transfer one layer to a serving platter.

To make the frosting: Beat the butter and confectioners' sugar together until smooth, then beat in brandy, to taste, and add milk a little at a time, beating until fluffy and smooth. Spread some of the frosting over the bottom cake layer, top with the second cake layer, and spread the remaining frosting over the top.

The Guy
Who
Liked Guys

Maybe I should have been tipped off by the expensive product in this guy's hair, since mine contained only sweat from the oven and a handful of forgotten bobby pins. Maybe I should have realized something was up by his catalog-quality outfit, since the sleeves of my cardigan were stained with frosting. Or maybe I should have gotten the hint when his circle of hyper-attractive guy friends appeared, who were all just as polished and put together as he was.

Before I knew it, they'd congregated around my cake in their unwrinkled shirts, asking polite questions and drawing me in with their mature conversational skills, voiced in dreamy baritones. It was like hanging out with civilian Ryan Gosling times four.

The guy I'd met first complimented my frosting and my eyes must have glazed over, betraying my blatant hetero attraction.

"Um, you should know we're all gay," he said gently, acknowledging his stunning friends. It was almost as if he expected me to take back the cake I'd just given to them.

"The cake is for everyone!" I said, waving a hand. "Of course I knew that." I hadn't.

They had really seemed straight—if only by the fact that they actually wanted to eat the cake.

THE MOST
SWINGING GUY
IN THE BAR
PROBABLY
SWINGS THE
OTHER WAY.

Peachy Keen Cake
with Minty Frosting

For the LGBT contingent, but can also be served up for a straight audience any day of the week.

For the cake:

1 cup (2 sticks/230 g) unsalted butter,
    at room temperature
1½ cups (300 g) sugar
3 large eggs
1 cup (280 g) pureed peaches
    (canned is fine; you'll need one
    15-ounce/425-g can of sliced
    peaches, drained)
½ cup (85 g) white chocolate chips,
    melted and cooled slightly
2½ cups (315 g) all-purpose flour
2 teaspoons baking powder
½ teaspoon salt

For the frosting:

¼ cup (50 g) sugar
2 large sprigs mint, torn
½ cup (1 stick/115 g) unsalted butter,
    at room temperature
4 cups (400 g) confectioners' sugar,
    sifted
1 to 2 tablespoons milk, if needed
Mint leaves, for garnish

To make the cake: Preheat the oven to 375°F (190°C). Butter two 9-inch (23-cm) round cake pans, line the bottoms with rounds of parchment paper, and dust the pans with flour, tapping out the excess.

Beat the butter and sugar together until creamy, then add the eggs, one at a time, scraping down the sides of the bowl. Add the peaches and the white chocolate.

In a separate bowl, combine the flour, baking powder, and salt. Working in batches, stir the flour mixture into the butter mixture. Divide the batter between the prepared pans.

Bake for 25 to 30 minutes, or until a toothpick inserted in the center of a cake comes out clean. Let cool for 5 minutes, then loosen the sides with a knife and invert onto wire racks to cool completely. Peel off the parchment and transfer one layer to a serving platter.

To make the frosting: In a small saucepan, combine the sugar, mint, and ¼ cup (60 ml) water and bring to a boil over medium heat. Let cool completely, then strain into a cup and discard the mint; you should have about 3 tablespoons of mint simple syrup.

Beat the butter and confectioners' sugar together until smooth, then beat in the syrup until fluffy and smooth, adding milk a little at a time, if needed. Spread some of the frosting over the bottom cake layer, top with the second cake layer, and spread the remaining frosting over the top and sides. Garnish with mint leaves.

The Guy
Who Took
My Cake

I must have given this guy the impression that I was very literally trying to get rid of my cake as, without a word, he took it from my hands and started offering it to other people at the bar, flat-out stealing my job. To stop him would have been to acknowledge there was a strategy behind the distribution, so I looked on helplessly as he worked the crowd, handing out the spoils of my labor. It was only when I saw him start advertising to a group of single girls that I felt it grounds to intercede, gently guiding him back to our table and reclaiming what was left of the beautiful cake.

While I privately resented him the rest of the time he sat with us, I had to give him credit for his tenacity.

I suppose this gesture should have been interpreted as helpful, not as an effort to overthrow my one-woman hostessing show. The guy had no way of knowing that this particular cake took me two-and-a-half hours to make and I only had fifteen to eighteen small- to medium-size pieces at my disposal.

I won't pretend I'm not subconsciously and constantly on the lookout for examples of gentlemanly behavior in our crumbling society, but the only thing I really needed this guy to do in that moment was sit still and eat my cake, preferably elaborating about how good it was.

Guys prove to be helpful when you least need them to be.

Melonhead Cake with Fizzy Frosting

For guys who don't understand your directions, intentions, or unspoken tactical plans.

For the cake:

½ cup (1 stick/115 g) unsalted butter, at room temperature

1 cup (200 g) sugar

1 cup (250 g) pureed cantaloupe or honeydew melon

4 large egg whites

½ teaspoon cream of tartar

3 cups (375 g) all-purpose flour

2 teaspoons baking powder

½ teaspoon baking soda

½ teaspoon salt

½ cup (120 ml) ginger ale

For the frosting:

½ cup (1 stick/115 g) unsalted butter, at room temperature

4½ cups (450 g) confectioners' sugar, sifted

3 tablespoons ginger ale

1 to 2 tablespoons milk, if needed

To make the cake: Preheat the oven to 375°F (190°C). Butter two 9-inch (23-cm) round cake pans, line the bottoms with rounds of parchment paper, and dust the pans with flour, tapping out the excess.

Beat the butter and sugar together until creamy. Add the melon.

In a separate bowl, using an electric mixer with the whisk attachment, whip the egg whites and cream of tartar together until soft peaks form, and set aside.

In a third bowl, combine the flour, baking powder, baking soda, and salt.

Working in batches, stir the flour mixture into the butter mixture, alternating with the ginger ale; stir until just combined. Stir in half of the egg whites to lighten the mixture, then gently fold in the remaining whites. Divide the batter between the prepared pans.

Bake for 20 to 25 minutes, or until a toothpick inserted in the center of a cake comes out clean. Let cool for 5 minutes, then loosen the sides with a knife and invert onto wire racks to cool completely. Peel off the parchment and transfer one layer to a serving platter.

To make the frosting: Beat the butter and confectioners' sugar together until smooth, then beat in the ginger ale until fluffy and smooth, adding a little milk if the frosting is too thick. Spread some of the frosting over the bottom cake layer, top with the second cake layer, and spread the remaining frosting over the top.

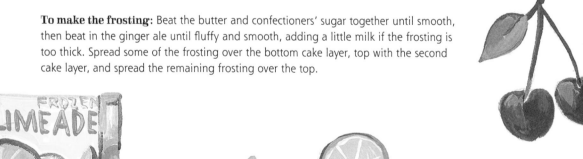

EMBARRASSING MOMENTS WORTH REVISITING

(that everyone should promptly forget)

(1) That time when everyone around us was on a date

(2) The first seventeen times I tried to order a drink at the bar and couldn't remember what I was supposed to do

(3) That time people discovered whole pieces of sweet potato in their cake because I hadn't properly mashed them

(4) That time I ran into one of my friends and was too embarrassed to tell him and his date what we were up to

(5) That time my friend tried to rip out my other friend's nose stud thinking it was a crumb

(6) That time when the cake tasted like cardboard and everyone was nice about it anyway

(7) That time when no one at the bar wanted any cake

(8) That time someone decided to kiss me for cake

(9) That time the bouncer wouldn't let me inside the bar

(10) That time I got frosting all over my dress

Chapter 5

Savory

Cakes for Meaningful Get-Togethers, Affirmative Encounters, and Reflective Solo Eating

After a year of so many newly acquired tastes—from batter to boys
to bars—here are the final cakes to accompany the stories that influenced
me the most, holding more weight than all the cakes I made combined.
What follows are surprising dessert combinations extracted from this
flavor-filled dating strategy—an experiment that taught me more about myself
than about baking, dating, or dudes. These are the cakes you make
to leave an impression—one you'll remember far longer than that guy
who asked for your number, and well after the last bite is gone.

The Guy Who Was a Hot Rocket Scientist

I almost fell over when this guy told me he was a rocket scientist. I thought maybe this was a joke, as rocket scientists were only supposed to be this good-looking when portrayed by actors on cable shows about spies.

Since I assumed he already had an equally brilliant and beautiful fiancée with whom he shared a small dog, I was beyond surprised when the rocket scientist not only sat down to have some cake, but put his arm around my chair while eating it. I considered this the next most appropriate move to putting his arm around me, which still meant things were moving pretty fast. "This is some legit cake," he pronounced, in what I can only describe as a husky, all-American genius voice.

It was like we were instantly best friends. I kept waiting for him to put together that I was far too quirky for his khaki-pants personality, that I knew about as much about science as he knew about decoupaging, that there was precious little overlap between our tribes, and that he could go ahead and go back to his table, but that moment never came. One thing led to another, and the two of us were playing the state capitals game with his friends and my friends until the bar closed at two in the morning.

We had bonded solely because he liked my baking and I liked to bake. The cake had leveled us to the same playing field, just two people reveling in a shared sugar high, and we were somehow—even if temporarily—a team.

The shortest distance between you and
a handsome genius can be computed
down to a single serving of cake.

Curry Carrot Cake
with Gingery Frosting

For exceedingly educated engineers, fiery chemists, and/or flirty rocket scientists.

For the cake:

½ cup (1 stick/115 g) unsalted butter,
   at room temperature
1 cup (200 g) sugar
3 large eggs
2 cups (210 g) grated carrots
2½ cups (310 g) all-purpose flour
2 teaspoons baking powder
½ teaspoon baking soda
½ teaspoon curry powder
½ teaspoon salt
1 cup (240 ml) plain yogurt

For the frosting:

2 cups (480 ml) Greek yogurt
½ teaspoon ground ginger
3 tablespoons honey
2 teaspoons lemon juice
Carrot shavings, for garnish

To make the cake: Preheat the oven to 375°F (190°C). Butter two 9-inch (23-cm) round cake pans, line the bottoms with rounds of parchment paper, and dust the pans with flour, tapping out the excess.

Beat the butter and sugar together until creamy, then add the eggs, one at a time, scraping down the sides of the bowl. Stir in the carrots.

In a separate bowl, combine the flour, baking powder, baking soda, curry powder, and salt.

Working in batches, stir the flour mixture into the butter mixture, alternating with the yogurt; stir until just combined. Divide the batter between the prepared pans.

Bake for 35 to 40 minutes, or until a toothpick inserted in the center of a cake comes out clean. Let cool for 5 minutes, then loosen the sides with a knife and invert onto wire racks to cool completely. Peel off the parchment and transfer one cake layer to a serving platter.

To make the frosting: Whisk the yogurt, ginger, honey, and lemon juice together. Spread some of the frosting over the bottom cake layer, top with the second cake layer, and spread the remaining frosting over the top and sides. Garnish with carrot shavings.

The Girl Who Didn't Have Cake for Her Birthday

She was surrounded by at least a dozen friends for her birthday, although there were no balloons, no presents, and there was definitely no cake. I couldn't help but find the whole situation rather socially unacceptable: who were these thoughtless friends of hers who hadn't thought to bake her a birthday cake or, at the very least, buy her one from the store? What was the point of even getting together to celebrate?

Seeing as how my entire cake still happened to be intact, I walked over and offered the birthday girl and her so-called party the whole thing, handing off this conveniently appearing dessert they hadn't ordered but had possibly meant to bring. About a third of the friends were guys, one of whom even generously bought me a Shirley Temple as thanks for the cake. But I wasn't doing this for them, of course—I was doing it for the girl.

Yes, I was straying from the mission—to first and foremost seek out suitable boyfriend material in the form of the oblivious cake-eaters—but when it really came down to it, I knew what was right.

Cakeless birthday parties are your call to arms.

Chocolate Chick-ory Cake with Dandelion Frosting

A gender-bending dessert for male and female cake-eaters alike.

For the cake:

1 cup (200 g) sugar plus 2 tablespoons
2 heads Belgian endive (chicory),
    leaves separated
½ cup (1 stick/115 g) unsalted butter,
    at room temperature
3 large eggs
2 cups (250 g) all-purpose flour
¾ cup (60 g) unsweetened cocoa
    powder, sifted
2 teaspoons ground roasted chicory
    root

2 teaspoons baking powder
½ teaspoon baking soda
½ teaspoon salt
1 cup (240 ml) sour cream

For the frosting:

8 ounces (1 block/225 g) cream
    cheese, at room temperature
½ cup (120 ml) heavy cream
1 cup (40 g) organic dandelion petals

To make the cake: Preheat the oven to 375°F (190°C). Butter two 9-inch (23-cm) round cake pans, line the bottoms with rounds of parchment paper, and dust the pans with flour, tapping out the excess.

In a small saucepan, combine 1 cup (240 ml) of water and the 2 tablespoons of sugar and place over medium heat. Add the endive leaves and cook until soft, about 5 minutes. Drain, pat dry with a paper towel, and chop. Set aside.

Beat the butter and remaining 1 cup (200 g) of sugar together until creamy, then add the eggs, one at a time, scraping down the sides of the bowl.

In a separate bowl, combine the flour, cocoa powder, chicory root, baking powder, baking soda, and salt.

Working in batches, stir the flour mixture into the butter mixture, alternating with the sour cream; stir until just combined. Stir in the endive. Divide the batter between the prepared pans.

Bake for 25 to 30 minutes, or until a toothpick inserted in the center of a cake comes out clean. Let cool for 5 minutes, then loosen the sides with a knife and invert onto wire racks to cool completely. Peel off the parchment and transfer one cake layer to a serving platter.

To make the frosting: Beat the cream cheese, cream, and dandelion petals together until fluffy. Spread some of the frosting over the bottom cake layer, top with the second cake layer, and spread the remaining frosting over the top.

ON GIRLS

A Study of Female Behavior in Bars

(1) That guy they're hanging out with might just be their brother.

(2) They're fast and smart enough to suddenly become teammates.

(3) Their cake compliments sway toward the short, sweet, and sincere.

(4) They'll watch your back when a weirdo's being weird . . .

(5) . . . but emerge from the woodwork if you're talking to their boyfriends.

(6) They're also probably wondering what happened to that bygone era when guys knew how to buy girls drinks without making things weird.

(7) There's always room for debate in what constitutes a "dress."

(8) Their vocal range reaches a special shrillness after midnight.

(9) They're more likely to take a piece of cake if they're working behind the bar.

(10) Bachelorette parties do, in fact, necessitate tiaras.

The Guy Who Asked for My Email Address

It was the kind of place where peanut shells coated the floor, and this guy was dancing in a three-piece suit. He and his friends were trying to keep up with the horrible house music, and I admired their attempts to look like they knew what they were doing. I waited for a break in the noise to ask if they wanted any cake, and all six of them ended up back at my table.

The guy in the suit sat and talked to me while his friends continued to gyrate around us, now far away from the music and staining their dress shirts with frosting. It turned out suit guy had clearly defined manners and a normal-person job, the equivalent of finding a unicorn cheerfully directing traffic along Hollywood Boulevard. He complimented the cake in between slow and courteous bites, and I appreciated his thoughtfulness coming through above the grating commotion of his friends. I felt like we were actually hitting it off.

His friends started drifting away, and it was clear he should probably get my phone number, or I should man up and ask for his. We were stalling, waiting for the other to take the lead, when he finally spoke up.

"Can I have your email address?" he asked.

It was with some comfort that I realized this part of the dating process must be as difficult for him as it had once been for me. This was like going back to dial-up AOL. At least I had graduated to the high-speed Internet way of asking someone for their number.

YOU MAY HAVE
TO WAIT FOR
GUYS TO CATCH
UP WITH YOUR
NEWLY ACQUIRED
CONFIDENCE.

Artichoked Cake with Balsamic Glaze

For young men who could use a shove forward in the dating arena, or a little encouragement taking the lead.

For the cake:

½ cup (1 stick/115 g) unsalted butter, at room temperature
1 cup (200 g) sugar
2 large eggs
1 (14-ounce/400-g) can artichoke hearts, drained and chopped
2 tablespoons grated Parmesan cheese
2 tablespoons minced scallions
1 tablespoon lemon juice
2½ cups (310 g) all-purpose flour
1 teaspoon baking powder
½ teaspoon salt

For the glaze:

2 cups (480 ml) balsamic vinegar
3 tablespoons brown sugar

To make the cake: Preheat the oven to 375°F (190°C). Butter two 9-inch (23-cm) round cake pans, line the bottoms with rounds of parchment paper, and dust the pans with flour, tapping out the excess.

Beat the butter and sugar together until creamy, then add the eggs, one at a time, scraping down the sides of the bowl. Add the artichokes, Parmesan, scallions, and lemon juice.

In a separate bowl, combine the flour, baking powder, and salt. Working in batches, stir the flour mixture into the butter mixture until just combined. Divide the batter between the prepared pans.

Bake for 25 to 30 minutes, or until a toothpick inserted in the center of a cake comes out clean and the tops are golden. Let cool for 5 minutes, then loosen the sides with a knife and invert onto wire racks to cool completely. Peel off the parchment and transfer one cake layer, bumpy-side up, to a serving platter.

To make the glaze: Put the vinegar and brown sugar in a wide saucepan and bring to a boil over high heat, then lower the heat and simmer for 20 to 30 minutes, until the mixture is thick enough to coat the back of a spoon and has reduced to about ¾ cup (180 ml). Drizzle the glaze generously over the bottom cake layer and top with the second cake layer. Drizzle the top with the remaining glaze, letting it drip down the sides.

The Guy
Who Seemed
Right

He'd driven up from the Westside to the Valley just to play pool with some buddies, what you out-of-towners should realize is a forty-five-minute to seventeen-hour nightmare of a commitment on any major freeway in Los Angeles. The fact that this guy had voluntarily made this journey on a Friday night made him seem like quite a good friend, which also seemed to imply he'd be quite a good boyfriend. He perked up when I asked if he wanted any cake. "Always," he said, which is always the right answer.

He mentioned he taught children music, and I tried not to lose myself in picturing all the precious recitals I could help him put on once we were ~~married dating~~ just getting to know each other. We ate a second piece of cake, bonding over a mutual Tami Taylor love, with all signs pointing to further action. But when it came time for us to go our separate ways, he just said good-bye, leaving me wondering if I had made some kind of error to derail us from planning to see each other again.

There are times when you head back into the bar to give the guy your number, those moments when you decide you have the power to try to make things go the way you want them to and aren't giving up just because maybe the other person isn't getting the message. But this wasn't one of those times. It was a night I accepted you can't force things that aren't supposed to happen. Some other girl was meant to help him plan all those student piano recitals.

MAKE PEACE
WITH THE CAKE
THAT DOESN'T RISE
AND FIND A
BETTER ONE
TO BAKE.

Squashed Blossom Cake with Pine Nut Frosting

For guys who are presumably good matches for you based on flimsy intel—just know a better match is out there.

For the cake:
¾ cup (1½ sticks/170 g) unsalted butter, at room temperature
1 cup (200 g) sugar
3 large eggs
1 cup (300 g) pureed cooked winter squash, such as butternut or pumpkin
⅓ cup (80 g) soft goat cheese
2½ cups (310 g) all-purpose flour
2½ teaspoons baking powder
½ teaspoon salt

For the frosting:
1 cup (240 ml) sour cream
1 tablespoon honey
2 tablespoons finely ground pine nuts
Squash blossoms, for garnish

To make the cake: Preheat the oven to 375°F (190°C). Butter two 9-inch (23-cm) round cake pans, line the bottoms with rounds of parchment paper, and dust the pans with flour, tapping out the excess.

Beat the butter and sugar together until creamy, then add the eggs, one at a time, scraping down the sides of the bowl. Add the squash and goat cheese.

In a separate bowl, combine the flour, baking powder, and salt. Working in batches, stir the flour mixture into the butter mixture until just combined. Divide the batter between the prepared pans.

Bake for 25 to 30 minutes, or until a toothpick inserted in the center of a cake comes out clean. Let cool for 5 minutes, then loosen the sides with a knife and invert onto wire racks to cool completely. Peel off the parchment and transfer one cake layer to a serving platter.

To make the frosting: Whisk the sour cream, honey, and pine nuts together. Spread some of the frosting over the bottom cake layer, top with the second cake layer, and spread the remaining frosting over the top. Garnish with squash blossoms, if desired.

NEVER WOULD I EVER

Things I Did Because of Cakebarring

(1) I called up Ryan Seacrest

(2) I appeared on national TV

(3) I started to drink an appropriate amount for a single young adult

(4) I wrote down my phone number for a guy who didn't ask for it

(5) I kissed a guy on the first date (and didn't care his hat hit me in the face on my way in)

(6) I played beer hockey with a slew of fraternity brothers

(7) I chatted up that actor I recognized

(8) I agreed with a radio host in Australia that I am moderately attractive

(9) I conveniently forgot the feedback that this experiment was antifeminist

(10) I wrote this book

The Guy
Who
Preferred Pie

He was sitting alone at a picnic table, smoking a cigarette and giving off a vampirey vibe that was coldly uninterested. I wasn't surprised to hear he had grown up in L.A., which can often give way to a general distaste for anything outside of it.

I offered him a piece of cake, but he said he was really more of a pie person.

"Have you ever been to Ramekin?" he asked.

"No," I said. "What's that?"

"We'll go there some time," he said, taking out his phone. "What's your number?"

Here's where I got lost. This guy hadn't wanted any cake, he wasn't planning to eat any cake, and we had only just met, about ninety seconds earlier. My hair wasn't especially clean, I wasn't particularly fond of the outfit I had chosen, and yet somehow this person was taking the necessary steps to ensure we would be spending more time together.

"Sure," I said, and gave him my number.

My social savvy may be limited to hosting, baking, and gaining the trust of small children, but I was smart enough to put together that this was a breakthrough, and I was supposed to follow through. Never in the history of the mission had someone expressed interest in dating me without the bait of the cake, and this moment held great significance. I wouldn't always need the cake as my crutch and my conversation starter; I would stay afloat in the dark and dismal dating waters past the end of the year.

SOMETIMES
YOUR BEST SELF
IS JUST
YOUR REAL ONE.

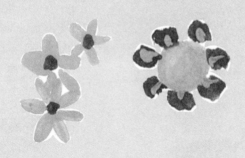

Sweet Potato Cake with Cauliflower Frosting

For people who aren't necessarily sweet, welcoming, or warm, but make conventionally nice gestures, e.g., inviting you out for dessert.

For the cake:

¾ cup (1½ sticks/170 g) unsalted
    butter, at room temperature
1 cup (220 g) brown sugar
3 large eggs
1 cup (290 g) cooked and pureed
    sweet potatoes (about 2)
1 teaspoon minced fresh rosemary
2½ cups (310 g) all-purpose flour
2 teaspoons baking powder
½ teaspoon salt
6 tablespoons (90 ml) sour cream

For the frosting:

8 ounces (1 block/225 g) cream cheese,
    at room temperature
1 cup (290 g) cooked and pureed
    cauliflower (about ½ small head)
Confectioners' sugar, for garnish

To make the cake: Preheat the oven to 375°F (190°C). Butter two 9-inch (23-cm) round cake pans, line the bottoms with rounds of parchment paper, and dust the pans with flour, tapping out the excess.

Beat the butter and brown sugar together until creamy, then add the eggs, one at a time, scraping down the sides of the bowl. Add the sweet potatoes and rosemary.

In a separate bowl, combine the flour, baking powder, and salt.

Working in batches, stir the flour mixture into the butter mixture, alternating with the sour cream; stir until just combined. Divide the batter between the prepared pans.

Bake for 20 to 25 minutes, or until a toothpick inserted in the center of a cake comes out clean. Let cool for 5 minutes, then loosen the sides with a knife and invert onto wire racks to cool completely. Peel off the parchment and transfer one cake layer to a serving platter.

To make the frosting: Beat the cream cheese and cauliflower together, either with an electric mixer or in a food processor, until smooth. If the frosting is too soft, put it in the refrigerator for a while to firm up before using. Spread some of the frosting over the bottom cake layer, top with the second cake layer, and spread the remaining frosting over the top. Sift the confectioners' sugar over the cake for garnish.

The Guy
Who I'd Grown
Up With

I could recognize his little-boy face in his man-size body from across the bar. We'd been paired up as waltz partners in the fourth grade, back when we were about the same size, a huge stroke of luck on my part since I thought he was cuter than JTT. Now he was much taller than I remembered, but I figured our height disparity had probably continued to increase after middle school, the last time we had seen each other.

I calculated which bad bangs period he had last been privy to and cringed; it was most likely from the height of my paralysis with boys, back when my posture was even worse than it is now and I was suffering from muffin top before people were calling it that. It was the beginning of my heightened uncertainty with male peers, a phase that had lasted until the start of this very experiment with cakes, when I had no choice but to loosen up because I'd thrown myself into the deep end of the being-with-boys pool.

Now I was a seasoned pro in the chatting-with-guys-in-bars department, having mastered all the eye contact and physical proximity practice that comes with it. I could talk to anyone, even this person who had seen me at my most unflattering, and ask if he wanted a piece of cake. I went up to say hello, and he nearly picked me up off the ground. Yes, he definitely wanted a piece of cake, and he gave me a kiss when he was finished.

YOU ARE NOT
THE SAME
AWKWARD PERSON
YOU WERE IN
MIDDLE SCHOOL,
EVEN IF YOU ARE
RUNNING AROUND
WITH CAKE
HOPING TO FIND
A BOYFRIEND.

Sweet Pea Cake with Crème Fraîche

For informal reunions with people from your past and unrequited childhood crushes.

For the crème fraîche:

1 cup (240 ml) heavy whipping cream
2 tablespoons cultured buttermilk

For the cake:

1 tablespoon olive oil
1 cup (170 g) diced onions
½ cup (1 stick/115 g) unsalted butter,
 at room temperature
1 cup (200 g) sugar
3 large eggs
1¾ cups (1 pound/455 g) pureed peas
2½ cups (310 g) all-purpose flour
2 teaspoons baking powder
½ teaspoon salt

To make the crème fraîche: Combine the cream and buttermilk in a glass jar and cover; let stand, undisturbed, on the counter for at least 8 hours or overnight to thicken. Refrigerate until ready to use.

To make the cake: Preheat the oven to 375°F (190°C). Butter two 9-inch (23-cm) round cake pans, line the bottoms with rounds of parchment paper, and dust the pans with flour, tapping out the excess.

In a small sauté pan, heat the oil over medium heat and add the onions. Cook, stirring frequently, until the onions are soft and translucent but not browned (add a little water and lower the heat if it does start to brown), about 10 minutes. Scrape onto a plate and let cool.

Beat the butter and sugar together until creamy, then add the eggs, one at a time, scraping down the sides of the bowl. Stir in the peas and onions.

In a separate bowl, combine the flour, baking powder, and salt. Working in batches, stir the flour mixture into the butter mixture. Divide the batter between the prepared pans.

Bake for 25 to 30 minutes, or until a toothpick inserted in the center of a cake comes out clean. Let cool for 5 minutes, then loosen the sides with a knife and invert onto wire racks to cool completely. Peel off the parchment and transfer one cake layer to a serving platter.

Spread some of the crème fraîche over the bottom cake layer, top with the second cake layer, and spread the remaining crème fraîche over the top.

The Guy Who Pointed Out the Obvious

He was a songwriter from Mississippi, so I guess it made perfect sense when he started elaborating on the texture of the cake like a poem, like a gosh-darn beautiful song. Several slices and a couple drinks later, we were old pals. I was emptying out my emotional purse, lamenting about the dating scene in Los Angeles. I confided that I'd really tried to put myself out there this year, but it hadn't exactly worked out yet.

"So why do you want a boyfriend so badly?" he asked.

I'd been taking cakes to bars for eleven months by this point. I'd bought enough sugar to stock an entire pastry school, spent enough time around drunk people to keep up with a college sorority, and subjected myself to a certain level of rejection and humiliation on a weekly basis. It was the most exhausting, adventurous, and fulfilling project I'd ever taken on. I was just as happy as I'd been when I started, if not happier, and I was just as single as I'd been at the beginning of the year.

"I don't think it's because I want a boyfriend so badly," I said. "Sometimes I just want some help carrying my groceries."

This big boyfriend void I'd envisioned suddenly seemed very filled by other purposeful space holders in the organizational chart of my life: friends, family, writing, working, baking, and using Instagram to immortalize oblivious boys eating cake in bars. If there had been any hole, I must have imagined it. There would be room created for the boyfriend when he showed up, and I wasn't trying to cram him in where he didn't belong.

MAYBE
YOU DON'T NEED
A BOYFRIEND
AFTER ALL.

Sage Cake with Ricotta Frosting

For wise advice-givers and unintentional mentors who help you reach important realizations, e.g., maybe you didn't need to bake fifty cakes to achieve a sense of wholeness in your life.

For the cake:

¾ cup (1½ sticks/170 g) unsalted
    butter, at room temperature
1 cup (200 g) sugar
3 large eggs
1 tablespoon lemon juice
2½ cups (310 g) all-purpose flour
2 teaspoons baking powder
½ teaspoon salt
2 tablespoons minced sage leaves
1½ cups (360 ml) ricotta cheese

For the frosting:

¾ cup (180 ml) heavy whipping cream
¾ cup (180 ml) ricotta cheese
Sage leaves, for garnish

To make the cake: Preheat the oven to 375°F (190°C). Butter two 9-inch (23-cm) round cake pans, line the bottoms with rounds of parchment paper, and dust the pans with flour, tapping out the excess.

Beat the butter and sugar together until creamy, then add the eggs, one at a time, scraping down the sides of the bowl. Add the lemon juice.

In a separate bowl, combine the flour, baking powder, salt, and sage.

Working in batches, stir the flour mixture into the butter mixture, alternating with the ricotta; stir until just combined. Divide the batter between the prepared pans.

Bake for 25 to 30 minutes, or until a toothpick inserted in the center of a cake comes out clean. Let cool for 5 minutes, then loosen the sides with a knife and invert onto wire racks to cool completely. Peel off the parchment and transfer one cake layer to a serving platter.

To make the frosting: In a chilled bowl, using a chilled whisk or electric mixer with the whisk attachment, whip the cream and ricotta until stiff peaks form. Spread some of the frosting over the bottom cake layer, top with the second cake layer, and spread the remaining frosting over the top. Garnish with sage leaves.

FURTHER READING

For Dating, Baking, and Bar-Hopping Inspiration

(1) *Heartburn* by Nora Ephron

Learn how to survive a disintegrating marriage, along with how to cook carbonara.

(2) *Are You My Boyfriend?* by Maria Peevey

Spin a wheel to find BF options that include the "It's Not You, It's Me Guy," and my personal favorite, "But He's Got a Great Personality Guy."

(3) *Ham Biscuits, Hostess Gowns, and Other Southern Specialties* by Julia Reed

Take a trip through the dreamy southland while picking up party tips and Reed's family recipes.

(4) *Drinking with Men* by Rosie Schaap

Join Schaap for her recollections of pubs, dives, and taverns, from New York and L.A. to Dublin, in this love letter to bars.

(5) *I Like You* by Amy Sedaris

Find out from the comedienne craft queen how to entertain for any event, from a gathering for the elderly to a birthday cake for your stepmother.

(6) *The Smitten Kitchen Cookbook* by Deb Perelman

Follow Perelman's witty instructions, and you'll make something incredible you thought you never could.

(7) *The Vintage Tea Party Book* by Angel Adoree

Up your hostessing game by learning how to style updos and sew aprons, in addition to baking treats like candy-striped meringues.

(8) *The Cake Mix Doctor* by Anne Byrn

Expand your cake horizons when you see how boxed mixes can transform into dozens of impressive desserts.

(9) *Help! I Can't Think of a Thing to Say* by Meg F. Schneider

Study this vintage gem for conversation starters like "You skate very well. How do you do that fancy backward move?"

(10) *Be Your Own Dating Service* by Nina Atwood

Should this cake thing not work out, listen to Atwood. She'll tell you everything you need to know.

THE END

Since we're being perfectly honest here, I'll admit a few more things. It's the least I can do, since you made it to the end of the book.

I am still that friend who hides during karaoke. I panic whenever I'm asked to find a partner in yoga class, and I go to great lengths to avoid high-fiving people. Next to running out of food at a dinner party, it is my single greatest fear to be selected for audience participation during an improv show, which means I always prefer to sit near the very back of the theater.

But throw me in a bar with a cake and I'll sing. Seat me next to a cute guy at dinner and I'll make so much eye contact, it will make your head spin. Give me a caketastrophe and I'll salvage it with frosting and charm. I won't sink, I'll swim—or at least tread water long enough to give it a real class-act effort.

Before this project, I would have blushed myself into a frenzy if I saw a guy I wanted to talk to at the grocery store. I really wouldn't have known what to say. Do you like that kind of cheese? Where do you get your parking validated? Is there any way we went to summer camp together? (I never went to summer camp.) Even if I don't have a cake in my hand, I've still got one pretty good icebreaker up my sleeve.

"This is going to sound crazy, but did I ever give you cake in a bar?"

Hopefully, that will at least get the conversation going, and I'll know where to take it from there.

ACKNOWLEDGMENTS

There's no way this book could have ever come together without the love and support of so many sugar monsters. Thank you to my amazing sister Madeline, who always gives the best writing advice of all. Thank you to my sweet Mom and Dad for believing in me, believing in this project, and spreading the good gospel of cakebarring throughout the southland. Thank you to my darling best friends Chrissy and Katy, the most incredible cheerleaders who lived, breathed, and ate this book with me. Thank you to my manager Mike De Trana for coming into my life with literal and emotional jumper cables last year. Thank you to Holly Dolce at Abrams for seeing the potential in my blog for a funny baking book, and to Cait Hoyt at CAA for hopping on the train shortly after. Thank you to my brilliant editor Camaren Subhiyah for her unfailingly excellent guidance, and the hugely talented Patricia Austin and Liana Krissoff for their respective recipe consulting. An enormous thank you to Darilyn Lowe Carnes and John Gall for their vision and art design, and to Jennifer Orkin Lewis for creating the gorgeous illustrations that make this book so beautiful and fun. Thank you to my inspiring Nashville mentors, Judy Lewis and Ann Patchett, for helping me steer my ship in life and on the page. Thank you to my surrogate family—Melanie, Larry, Evie, and Henry—for all their generosity and warmth, and to my bosses—Rabih, Fernando, and Chris—for my day job and the occasional boy advice.

Thank you to my saintly friends who went cakebarring at all hours of the night that year, having their ankles licked and nose studs nearly ripped out:

Ginny, John W., Dave, Marcella, Alex, Elizabeth G., Ashley G., Stacy, Laurie, Savannah, Jen S., Kirsten, Sean, Andy, Nick, Monica B., Vlada, Katie R.B., Katie E.B., Georgia, Chris, Sarah, Emily A., Andra, Carrie, Natalie, Sam, Becky, Vin, Petra, Katie O., Liz, Michelle, Ashlei, Val; my cousins Jobie, Laura, Lindsey, Amy and Emily G.; my sweet Nana Myrna for her baking help; Jon A., Emma, Jenny, Annabeth, Connor, Mike N., Emily C., Jen B., Lauren O., Mara, Tobie, Laura Beth, James, Anna Z., Mary Claire, Rita, Dean, Christine, Hunter Claire, Adam, Ziona, Mallory, Neely, Anna F., Nikki, Dani, Lauren B., Justine, Kathryn, Peter, Heidi, Stephanie, Jalika, Rachel, Allison, Kathi, Talia, Monica V., Marco, Ashley A., Alicia, Christiana, Jonathan, Iliza, Mike B., Jennie, Avery, Hannah, Claire, Elizabeth S., Meagan, Kelly, Russell, and Kathleen.

I couldn't have done it without you guys.

And last but certainly not least, thank you to all the boys who ate the cake (or didn't eat the cake), and thank you to Jamie, the last boy I baked for.

INDEX